THE PERSONAL CFO

THE PERSONAL CFO

THE SECRET TO
GETTING MORE
OUT OF YOUR
MONEY AND YOUR LIFE

KYLE WALTERS

LIONCREST
PUBLISHING

THE PERSONAL CFO

The Secret to Getting More Out of Your Money and Your Life

ISBN   978-1-5445-1101-6 *Hardcover*

   978-1-5445-1100-9 *Paperback*

   978-1-5445-1099-6 *Ebook*

For Claire, Olivia, and My Astronaut

CONTENTS

INTRODUCTION

When I have enough money, I want to learn the intricacies of estate, tax, investment, and insurance planning.

—SAID NOBODY, EVER

After fifteen years and thousands of meetings, I owe my clients an apology.

Throughout my career, I've tried to spread my passion for finance to my clients, often overexplaining, pontificating, and "educating" extremely successful individuals on the nuances and complexities of how the endless web of finance works.

Everyone is wired a certain way; we all have a predisposition to different things. I was born with a predisposition to numbers. The topic of finance first drew me in as a six-year-old boy when I read *The Berenstain Bears' Trouble with Money*. I read it over, and over, and over again. I was fascinated, even at such a young age. When I was working with numbers, I was in my territory—a natural state, so to speak.

In fact, anything outside of finance felt unnatural, and even after all these years, I'm still easily excitable about it.

Even now, as an adult, when I go on vacation, I'll take financial literature to read as opposed to a best-selling novel. I simply don't enjoy reading for what other people call "pleasure." It's torture to me—I've tried. I take financial literature because it's much more interesting, and because there's no bottom to the rabbit hole when it comes to the financial world; there's always more to learn.

My obsession with finance would swell during my meetings with clients, and I would talk about all sorts of financial concepts and how exciting I thought it was. Even on the phone with clients, I would keep them on the line for an hour. It wasn't until a few years ago that I realized my clients were only humoring me. The reality was they had little to zero interest in the topic, and I'd even go so far as to say some *hated it*. They sat there because they liked me, not because they wanted to know about anything I had to say.

It's like taking your car to the mechanic and letting him

spend hours explaining the intricate details of what's wrong with your crankshaft or carburetor system. Unless you're really into cars, you probably don't care.

For years, I was that overly excited and passionate mechanic. My wife would hear me on a call and say: "You shouldn't talk so much; they don't care as much as you think they do."

It took me years to realize that not everyone is wired the way I am. The clients I met with over those meetings weren't there for more information; information is infinite. They weren't there to share my passion for finances, either; they were there for advice. They were in my office to find a partner they trusted. They were looking for someone to help get them where they wanted to go financially so they could spend valuable time where *their* passion lies. I feel as though I've done a disservice to my clients because of this, so I'd like to apologize.

I'm sorry.

The reason I've written this book is because I've been doing it wrong over the last fifteen years. It has taken me a long time because, frankly, I am in an industry among others who are equally passionate about what we do, so we're all making the same mistakes, which is to overeducate and "empower" our clients and teach them what we've spent years studying, understanding, and implementing.

This idea for advisors to impose all of their knowledge and passion onto their clients needs to change, and I hope this book starts that conversation. I wrote this book to shift the dynamic between the financial services industry and the clients we serve. What we need to do as an industry instead is focus on helping clients clearly identify where they are now, where they want to go, and how they get there.

The reality is that most people aren't obsessed with finance; most aren't even mildly interested. In fact, looking back at my meetings, everyone was looking for permission to say, "I don't care. Please just look at what I'm doing financially and tell me what I need to do to reach my goals."

And that's okay. There's absolutely nothing wrong with that.

UNREALISTIC EXPECTATIONS

Our modern culture has created an unrealistic expectation that we as individuals are supposed to know everything, especially about our finances. This proliferation of information that grants us access to everything has been misconstrued into a belief that we are "empowered" to make every important decision in our lives. The problem, however, is that we don't know how to interpret all the accessible information.

If I were diagnosed with a tumor in my leg, for example, and wanted to perform surgery on myself, I could technically find all the necessary information on the internet and do it myself. I can find all that information right now, on my phone. I can read every piece of data, watch videos, memorize the instructions, purchase the instruments needed—everything. But to actually attempt the surgery without formal training or experience would be insane. Just because I have the information from the internet and can buy the tools from Amazon doesn't mean I am capable of performing surgery.

The challenge with applying the same concept to personal finance is *you won't know if you're killing yourself.*

Our society has changed dramatically since the dawn of the internet. Thirty years ago, when people didn't have access to every bit of available information, they talked to somebody they trusted. They sought answers from experts. They found professionals who provided services for their needs.

The information age has off-loaded a great deal of work on the individual—work previously done by others with expertise or specialists. We feel as though we have to do the job of ten different people while trying to keep up with our lives, our family, our friends, our careers, our hobbies, and our interests.

Because we have access to everything, we feel as though we should be doing things that don't fall under our interests or our expertise. This is why everybody is busier than ever—they have adopted additional roles they feel pressured to take on.

UNDERSTANDING MOTIVATION AND THE DIYF

A major reason we feel the need to become experts in everything, especially personal finance, is due to nonstop badgering from the media. The financial journalists you see on television and read in print do not publish material to help you; their goal is for you, the consumer, to keep coming back for more.

Magazines like *Money Magazine* and news channels like CNBC are two of many media outlets I like to tag under the DIYF (do it yourself finance) culture.

These DIYF magazines put out, effectively, twenty articles every month with hooks like, "Make the most of your money," "Optimize your retirement," and "Take control of your personal finances."

Here's the deal: having twenty new strategies or ideas for you to act on every month is unrealistic. Think about it. That would be 240 new options, strategies, and concepts for you to read about and implement to your portfolio—every year. Financial decisions, like the majority of significant decisions, should be principle-driven. Principle-driven decisions are based on things we know are true, and they don't change day to day or year to year. Financial DIYF news channels have to come up with flashy headlines to grab your attention regarding your finances because they want you to keep coming back for more.

Think about the motivation behind these DIYF magazines. The publication's job is to sell magazines, not provide you with good advice. They are not compensated by how successful you are financially. They are compensated by how many ads they sell, so their motivation is to garner as many eyeballs on each issue as possible, which means they have to come up with content and reasons for you to pick up and pay for the magazine. In essence, it's a financial tabloid, like the *National Enquirer*. Thankfully, most people know that the contents of the *National Enquirer* are not true; most people know it's an entertainment publication.

When financial news mediums publish headlines like, "Secure Your Retirement with These Top Four Funds," I can't help but laugh. How many people are reading this article? These are the four funds that will help every single reader across all generations and risk tolerances to achieve their individual goals? Who's writing these stories? These articles are not written by financial experts; they're written by journalists. You're taking advice from a writer, *not a financial expert*.

My favorite headlines are the ones where some sort of "secret" is exposed.

"The Secret to Real Estate Investing Success."

"The Secret to Tax-Free Giving."

"The Secret to Retiring Rich without Stocks."

In the investment world, the only way a secret works is if no one knows about it. If someone has a secret to their success, the reason why they've found success is because they've kept it a secret. If a secret is divulged, not only is it not a secret anymore, but it probably won't work anymore. These articles are headlined by design to grab your attention so you continue reading the article.

Another favorite is when an article draws you in with a big name.

"Ten Best Money Tips of All Time from Warren Buffett."

"Michael Bloomberg's Top Five Rules for Success."

Warren Buffet or Michael Bloomberg didn't write those articles. Somebody wrote an article about them, which is not the same thing. A journalist is writing about somebody who's wealthy, and pulling you in with the message, "This is probably what they did."

Unfortunately, people read these articles and then make decisions based on what they read. This is problematic because these articles are too broad, and they don't take into consideration the specific goals and needs of the individual reader. Doctors don't go around giving specific medical advice in medical journals, because every patient is different, and it's risky to do so. What doctors can (and do) write about, however, are general principles for good health, which include getting enough sleep, drinking lots of water, eating a balanced diet, and exercising.

The media doesn't work like that.

Now, I'm not claiming that everything ever published in financial magazines is wrong; you just have to understand the motivation behind the method. They are designed as entertainment to get you to read them. You should not, however, make any major decisions based on what you read.

Everything in our lives today is competing for our attention. Everything is published or programmed with blinking lights and "like buttons" to satisfy the immediate gratification that our goldfish attention spans crave. Let's look at DIYF news stations on television. These news stations are designed to grab your attention, and they do so by inducing fear. I could turn on any DIYF channel at any time during the day and see the words "Breaking News" on the screen, followed by a headline. How is that possible?

"Breaking News! GM's Earnings Are in Line with Estimate."

How does that qualify as breaking news? *There is no breaking news that will impact your long-term goals.*

In our office, we do not play DIYF channels on the television in our lobby, because it's panic inducing by design. Instead, we play travel videos of the Galapagos (my personal favorite travel destination)—because who doesn't like turtles? I often tell clients that nothing on DIYF shows will ever have an impact on their long-term goals. These stations are designed to sell advertisements and are programmed with content to keep viewers watching. That's why you'll see two individuals with opposing views talk about a topic—to entertain the viewers. These individuals are equally passionate about the topic, and it's likely that neither is right or wrong. These programs are streamed for fun, to entertain the public, and they usually do not even offer any real-life solutions. Another example is when these DIYF shows find people who claim they are "experts" and have them share their opinions about how the market will perform in the future. One person thinks it will go up; the other thinks it will go down. This, to me, is entertainment, but these DIYF news stations present it as fact—information you should use to make financial decisions. It's not. They just want viewers to tune in and watch.

Unfortunately, the financial industry is drowning in this type of news media that constantly tells people what to do financially without understanding the bigger picture. They don't care about you; they care about selling advertisements (which doesn't make them bad, either; you just have to understand their motivation).

I'm here to tell you that you don't have to subscribe to these DIYF platforms. I opened this chapter with a quote no one I know has ever said: "When I have enough money, I want to learn the intricacies of estate, tax, investment, and insurance planning."

Again, that's *okay*.

SHIFTING EMPOWERMENT

There are two types of empowerment: one is to be empowered to do it yourself; the other is to empower someone else to do it.

A recent poll asked the general public, "If you were diagnosed with cancer, would you want to choose your treatment?" Sixty-seven percent said yes. When they asked the same question to people who were actually diagnosed with cancer, however, only 12 percent wanted to choose their treatment.

People like the concept of having more choices, because they think more choice is better. When reality sets in and the rubber meets the road, however, more choices—past a certain point—do not help. A doctor doesn't approach someone with cancer and say, "Here's a list of fifty cancer treatment options. Look it over and let me know which one you'd like me to administer." That would never happen. Even if the doctor showed the patient only three options, the patient would still ask, "What would you do? Which one of the three do you recommend?"

When it comes down to it, people like the idea of choice, because it gives them a sense of do-it-yourself empowerment. This empowerment surrounds us through the DIYF channels with the constant messages, "You can do everything yourself," and "Take control of your life." The empowerment to do it yourself is propaganda that has been pushed onto us for the better part of the last decade, and I want to change that. I'd like to *shift* the empowerment to the second kind—empowering someone else to do it for you.

Both options are available to you. You can choose either, and neither one is wrong. You can be empowered to do things yourself, but you are trading your time and energy by doing so. What else could you be doing? It all boils down to the question of time. With everything happening in your life, what do you want to spend your time on? There's nothing wrong with empowering somebody else to handle the things you don't want to handle. That way, you can do the things you want to do.

Growing up in the industry, I felt the need to teach my clients everything I knew because I thought I was empowering them. I was sharing my knowledge because I thought it would make them feel better if they understood all the moving parts. Not only did I realize that it's not possible for me to do so within the time I spend with each client, but I realized that I wasn't empowering them at all. I was only overwhelming them.

Nowadays, I ask clients, "How much do you want to know?" They usually answer by saying something along the lines of, "I just want to know as much as I need to know to make the best decision possible." *That's it.*

People who are selling you on the first empowerment are not your advisors. They do not know you. They're selling you the idea that you should do this yourself when you know you shouldn't. It's infuriating as an advisor, because this isn't fair to people. They don't know they're being duped.

Advisors who are overeducating clients by saying, "Here are your options; please let me know which one you want," are just lazy. What are they really doing? They're passing the buck for responsibility and accountability. If the choice you make ends up being detrimental, they say, "Well, you chose to do that."

That is not an advisor. An advisor is accountable for helping you get where you need to go—and not by giving you options. An advisor is a partner.

If you decide to DIYF, ask yourself these three questions: Do I understand it? Do I like learning about it? Do I want to trade my time on it?

Do I understand it? Is this something that I feel is one of my core competencies (as in, do you understand it more than other people)?

Do I like learning it? Is this something I would do in my free time? If I didn't have to do this, would I do it?

Do I like doing it? Would it be considered a hobby that I enjoy doing?

Do I want to trade my time on it? Where do I put my most precious resources? Am I willing to trade those to do this?

If you answer yes to these three, then great! But everyone has a limited capacity for time and attention. I don't want to trade my life for things I don't care about, especially if somebody else can do them for me. And that's what time is: **trading life.** I'm trading a part of my life to help others with their finances because I get it and because I love it. I don't replace my own roof, because I don't have the skills or wherewithal to do so. I delegate as much as possible so I can spend my time on what's more important to me.

This empowerment myth has made people devalue their time. They don't account for the fact that they're spending X amount of time on something they're not an expert in, in an industry that is constantly changing.

I want to shift this sense of empowerment. I want to empower you to find the solution so you can go do what you actually enjoy. I want people to feel empowered to say, "I don't care about this stuff, but I know it all needs to be done. It needs to be done with excellence and account-ability, but I don't need to know the nitty-gritty details."

Some advisors may argue that their clients want to know all the details. Maybe they do, but I've never met someone who does. And I think if I met with them, they would eventually admit that they don't care, either. They're only saying they care because the advisors make it seem like they're supposed to care.

During introductory meetings when I first sit down with a client, 90 percent of them make comments like, "I know I should be better educated on this," or "I know I should learn more about this." They come in and they're ashamed and embarrassed for not being an expert. They often start the meeting by apologizing. Not only is it a reflection of the empowerment myth, it's a mindset that has been imposed on them by the industry and the media. It's the reason they feel confused and overwhelmed, because they feel as if they're supposed to want to understand these foreign concepts.

In general, these are accomplished and successful people, yet they say, "I should know more about this." No, you don't have to. You don't need to know all the intricacies of this.

If you're doing your own financial planning in the beginning, it's not a big deal. You're learning, and even if you make mistakes (and you probably will), they're unlikely to leave a large impact. Eventually, you'll get to a point where you will say, "I can't keep practicing on myself. I need a professional." Compare this to falling and scraping your knee. It might hurt a little, but it's not a big deal. Clean it up, put a Band-Aid on it, and you're good. You're not going to lose the leg. If you break your leg, however, you're going to need a doctor.

When the stakes are low, it's okay to make mistakes. Scrape your knee, and put a Band-Aid on. But once complexity rises, your issues change, the stakes become much higher, and the decisions you make become more important.

THE MOST VALUABLE RESOURCE

The cost of a thing is the amount of what I call life, which is required to be exchanged for it immediately or in the long run.

—DAVID HENRY THOREAU

When you're committing your time to something, you're spending life. Time is our ultimate nonrenewable resource. When it all comes down to it, when D-Day hits us all, what's the only thing people wish they had more of? Time. Right now, we squander it because we don't view it as a finite resource.

Where do you want to spend this valuable resource? Is it on the intricacies of estate, tax, investment, and insurance planning? I doubt it. Instead, people say, "I want to spend the *right amount of time* to get comfortable with the decision-making process, and then I want to spend *as little time as possible* afterward." Spending as little time as possible in one area means they can spend as much time as possible in the areas they care about.

What is the price you're paying? What is the price of empowerment? What are other things you would be doing with that time? Is it volunteering? Is it traveling the world? Is it working on your business? Is it spending time with your grandkids?

THE PERSONAL CFO

Most companies have a CEO, a leader who controls the vision of the company (where are we going?) and the values (why are we going there?). They allocate resources and identify areas that are important and need the most attention, all while making sure the company is profitable.

Most companies also have a CFO working alongside the CEO to move the company toward its goals. The CFO understands the CEO's vision and values; takes the strategic direction of the company, where they want to go; and supports it by offering insight and context to help make better financial decisions. The CFO and CEO make a great team and, working together, they can accomplish great things.

After many, many years in the industry, and through the mistakes I've made, I've realized that the same roles can— and should—be applied to our personal lives. Once we get to a certain stage in our careers, complexity can rise to the point where family units are effectively personal corporations, so they need the same roles that companies have.

I wanted to write this book to introduce the benefits you can get out of a relationship with a personal CFO and what that looks like.

You are the CEO of your life. You decide what you want to do in the future, and how to get there. You have assets, liabilities, income, and expenses. Unfortunately, most personal CEOs don't have a personal CFO. Most personal CEOs don't have someone who can say, "Here's what these financial decisions mean to you, your family, your company." Without a CFO, more often than not, your personal financial landscape isn't working as well as it could.

Both of these roles are necessary, but they are vastly different. *You are the CEO; you cannot delegate that. Only you know what you want in life.*

Unfortunately, most personal CEOs are also the CFO— which can be overwhelming. Based on everything that we're going to talk about in this book, if you don't know immediately who that person is, you do not have one, which means you are doing both roles.

The good news is that you can delegate the role of the CFO. By doing so, not only does a personal CFO help you make better financial decisions, but more importantly, you get your life back.

WHO IS THIS BOOK FOR?

This book is for those who have found success and are busy with their careers and families. This book is for those who have, throughout their lives, experienced failures, learned from them, dusted off their shoulders, and moved on. This book is also for those who are financially independent and who want to spend their time pursuing their purpose instead of managing the financial minutiae their success has created.

This book is about a relationship. It's about shifting the empowerment from doing everything yourself to finding a trusted partner. It's about setting proper expectations for the people we work with because successful people expect a certain level of accountability.

This book is about saving you time and giving you the ability to become the CEO of your own life. This book is for the person who is hanging their head right now saying,

"I know I need to learn more about this." You really don't. It's okay if you don't care, because with a proper partner, you don't need to care.

We used to be in the place where we needed more information. As times change and as our world evolves, we don't need that anymore. Now we need an integrator, a catalyst, and an advocate. The DIYF likes to throw everything back on the client, as if they're supposed to know how to put it all together.

This book is about raising the level of expectations that people should have of the advisors whom they work with.

This book *is not* a "how-to" book. This book won't provide you any to-do lists, nor will you find any financial strategies within these pages. At the end of this book, you should understand what to look for in a trusted advisor, a partner, a personal CFO.

This book won't teach you how to grow your portfolio to some arbitrary amount. Wealth is the ability to fully experience life. What does experiencing life mean to you? *That* is the question that should be addressed. How much more fulfilled would you be if you could spend your time on that question, rather than on all the minutiae of properly managed personal finances? That is the conversation you should have with your advisor.

In the following chapters, I will introduce the concept of the personal CFO and explain the benefits it can bring to your life.

Let's get started.

PART

I

THE POWER

CHAPTER ONE

INFORMATION OVERLOAD

If information was the answer, then we'd all be billionaires with perfect abs.

—DEREK SIVERS

The iPhone today is more powerful and has more computing power than NASA had when they landed on the moon.

Information is at our fingertips on computers we carry around in our pockets, and everywhere we go, we're bombarded with more and more information. If you start feeling sick, you Google your symptoms. If you're watching a film, you can look up what the lead actor ate for breakfast that day on Instagram. If you have a question, you type it into a search engine, and in a matter of seconds, hundreds of web links are listed for you to browse. If I wanted to learn about rocket science, I could. There is nothing we encounter today that we can't look up online. Everything is searchable. *Everything.*

Information is important, but what people do with that information is paramount. People don't have a problem with information; they have a problem with application. They struggle with the application part because it's unclear whether the information brings any personal significance to their lives. All of this information—especially when there is so much of it—is often generic, and there is no filter for us to see if it means anything to us specifically.

There is an abundance of information, but the thing is, we don't need more information. We don't need more data. We need more knowledge and wisdom.

THE DIKW TRIANGLE

Knowledge is knowing that a tomato is a fruit, wisdom is not putting it in a fruit salad.

—MILES KINGTON

The DIKW triangle reflects the hierarchy of how we interpret and make decisions. It stands for **data, information, knowledge,** and **wisdom.**

Data consists of pure and simple facts, in no particular order. Information is a refinement of that data—the value we extract from it. *What does it mean?* Knowledge derives from filtering information, using it strategically to achieve objectives. *What does this mean for me?* And wisdom is the capacity to choose those objectives that are consistent with one's values within a larger context. *What do I do now?* Or in other words, *now what?*

The first two are context independent; the latter two reflect an advanced level of understanding and application.

We're often compelled to take action at the bottom of the triangle, by data and information. We don't run it all the way up when we are making important decisions. We need to run it all the way up the triangle. Give it meaning, then give it context, then understand what it could mean to you. We're spending all of our time in the murk of data and information, which is problematic because it always changes. There's never a way to get enough of it, and it doesn't do you any good, because when you finally figure out a way to apply the data or information, it's already changed again. Think back to the various breaking-news outlets. They want you to watch the station, and to keep you watching, they offer content that changes every day.

Thanks to the World Wide Web, people believe they must do more because they have access to everything. The implication is that you should find the data and the information, and then do everything yourself. This can be a challenge.

The real problem lies in the application: How do you apply all this data and information? We used to apply knowledge and wisdom to making decisions, but now we're applying far more data and information, which only makes things overwhelming.

The abundance of information also plays into our immediate-gratification needs, and we become consumed by it. The dopamine release of finding information grants us immediate satisfaction.

Whereas information is fluid and constantly changing, knowledge and wisdom reflect core values and principles—these don't change. They stand the trials of time. That's why certain texts written hundreds of years ago by authors like Plato and Sun Tzu still apply today. When Julius Caesar wrote about the Roman Empire, he wasn't gossiping about what had happened on a certain day. That would be data and information. Instead, he spoke to universal human concepts that can be applied across time, regardless of technological advancements. He was writing about knowledge and wisdom—and the majority of what he wrote about still applies today.

Experience is the teacher of all things.

—JULIUS CAESAR

Knowledge and wisdom can—and should—be applied to

your decisions, whether you're buying a car, buying a new house, or saving money to send your kids to college. Your decisions should be guided by principles and values, not constantly changing information according to what you read on the internet.

Unfortunately, we're not as focused on timeless principles. Getting from information to knowledge and wisdom takes time and effort. That's why we have doctors, scientists, and Olympic athletes. They've spent the time and energy to become the best in their respective fields. They say it takes ten thousand hours to master a craft. We as humans don't have the capacity to be experts in everything. When we aren't experts in a certain field, the application of data and information can be dangerous.

If someone has information but doesn't know how to apply it, they're going to try to apply it anyway, sometimes incorrectly. They won't know what it might mean for them, or what it means in a broader context. With access to information, they're more likely to feel confident that they can do it on their own.

A doctor can give you endless data, but it will remain meaningless to you. When she applies context to information, she can connect the dots and tell you what that data means to you, specifically. Based on the *information*, here's what it means for you, the *knowledge*, and then here's what you should do about it, which is *wisdom*.

Principles don't change. Let's look at weight loss as an example. How do you get into shape? There is an endless amount of information about weight loss out there. We can talk for hours about calories, food, diets, strength training, and so on. When you jump to the principles behind weight loss, the fundamental rules are don't eat processed food, drink lots of water, and take the stairs.

Principles apply now and they'll apply in fifty years because, intuitively, they make sense. If a principle doesn't apply in ten years, it's not a principle.

TRUST ISSUES

Some people have a hard time trusting others. They don't trust anybody but themselves to be in control, which plays into our overwhelming information-centric research culture. They feel the need to do everything themselves, which consumes their time and energy on things they don't even want to do.

Before the internet and the onset of information overload, if someone woke up with a throbbing toothache, that person would call upon a dentist and ask him to take a look. If someone woke up with incredible stomach pains, they'd immediately make an appointment with their doctor to find out what was wrong. People used to call upon experts to develop a diagnosis and prescribe a treatment. Today, Dr. Google answers our questions.

Unfortunately, Google never says, "Don't sweat it. Go see your doctor." Instead, it shows you a list of what could potentially be wrong with you—and somehow cancer always lands on the list. You have an eye infection? Cancer. Now you're more anxious and nervous because you think you're dying, when in reality, all you have to do is talk to an expert.

Heaven forbid you click on "images." When you're self-diagnosing, *never look at the images.*

All the information Google spits out at us only makes things worse. It makes it worse for you and for the medical professional who not only has to diagnose and prescribe a treatment for whatever it is that's ailing you, but now has to calm you down and unwind everything you "learned." When was the last time you went to see a doctor with a complex issue and said, "Doc, here's exactly what I think is wrong," and you were right?

Less than people think.

I'm guilty of Googling my symptoms too. In my thirty-seven years, I've never been right—not once (that was hard for me to admit)!

Every moment you spent worrying and thinking about what you read on the internet didn't help, because you didn't know how to apply the information correctly. You can diagnose, but you can't prescribe. What you need to focus on is how to clearly articulate the problem so that any personal information becomes more relevant to the person who knows how to apply it.

The diagnosis is extremely important, so being able to clearly articulate the goal or the problem is where you should be spending your time. When I'm talking to a travel agent, I need to clearly articulate the type of vacation I want. If I only say I want to vacation on the beach, that's too vague. That could be California, Fiji, or even Antarctica. I need to clearly articulate my problem and my goal.

DECISIONS SUFFER

When you think you have to do everything, decisions suffer as a result because (a) you're overwhelmed with the amount of information available, and (b) it'll take too much time for you to reach the level of knowledge to make sound decisions.

Our culture of information overload has left us less fulfilled than ever. You're not allowed to disconnect anymore, because the workhorse mentality is a badge of honor.

We're confusing research with the front page of the search engine. People think Yahoo Answers is research. Professionals don't answer questions online, because they know better—they can't prescribe without a diagnosis. Doctors, rocket scientists, and financial experts are not writing recommendations online, because they don't know anything about you—and recommendations change based on *you*.

The worst thing about online advice is that other users—who have no idea what they're talking about—rate the answers. They're not experts. In the land of the blind, the one-eyed man is king. You don't need to be on that island. Until an expert says, "Let's talk about you; I need to have a firm understanding of you, your family, your goals and objectives," nothing can be applied.

If somebody tries to give you recommendations before they know you, be careful. No professional works that way, whether she's a consultant, financial advisor, doctor, or architect. Unless they fully understand how everything would correlate with your goals, objectives, and family, application cannot happen.

ILLUSION OF EFFICIENCY

Since our culture expects us to do so much on our own, when someone does hire an expert to take care of such services, they're looked down upon. They're viewed as lazy. We're living in an anti-concierge society. Most successful people are expert delegators because they know they don't have the time or energy to spend—nor would they want to. They don't want to spend the time gathering information, because they know they won't become extremely good at applying it—and if they're not going to be great at it, why bother? They only spend time on what they absolutely love. They're going to spend their time on things they want to spend time on, whether that's related to their business or not.

They focus on the things they want to be trading their life for, and then delegate the rest. Delegate or flip the empowerment switch, not to empower yourself to do it, but to empower someone else to do it for you.

CHAPTER TWO

DECISION FATIGUE

In 2000, psychologists Sheena Iyengar and Mark Leger published a study that argued that more choices aren't always better. They set up a table in a gourmet food store in an upscale part of town and gave out samples of different flavored jams. Customers could taste each flavor and were given a coupon for a dollar off if they purchased one. One day, the customers had the option to choose between six flavors of jam. The next day, customers could try twenty-four.

People flocked to the table on the day twenty-four types of jam were offered, far more than the day with only six. When it came to buying the jam, however, more wasn't better. Thirty percent of the people who tasted from the smaller batch ended up buying a jar of jam. In contrast, when given twenty-four options, only 3 percent of people bought a jar. People were ten times more likely to make a decision when there were fewer options on the table.

When given six options—say strawberry, grape, blueberry, apricot, lemon, and habanero—the human brain can distinguish between them fairly easily, and it's relatively simple to make a decision. When given twenty-four options, however, the differences become subtle, and it's more difficult to make a decision. When pressed with so many options, your brain doesn't know how to weigh them, it becomes paralyzed, and you end up not choosing anything at all.

This is called decision fatigue.

Decision fatigue has penetrated our day-to-day lives—from deciding what to wear, what to eat, and, yes, what you should do with your personal finances.

For some reason, our modern society takes pride in all the choices we have. According to a 2014 *Consumer Report* article, at a single supermarket today, you'll find twenty-seven different Crest toothpastes. Frankly, I'd rather there just be one. At any given grocery store, there are twenty-nine types of chicken soup, 175 different salad dressings—of which sixteen are Italian—and an entire aisle dedicated to 275 types of cereal—with seven different types of Cheerios! That many choices worry me a little bit. Every time you make a decision—no matter how seemingly insignificant—it uses up brain-space and will-power that you could be using on other, more important decisions. Do you really need to spend your limited energy choosing between twenty-seven flavors of toothpaste? I certainly hope not (but don't forget to floss!).

ENDLESS CHOICES, ENDLESS PROBLEMS

Choice is supposed to be liberating, but in reality, it can sometimes be debilitating. I referenced in the first chapter how only 12 percent of cancer patients actually want to choose their treatment. A choice with one option is easy—yes or no. When there are three choices presented, making a choice is still relatively easy and straightforward. But when we are tasked with making a choice out of an option of ten, twenty, thirty, or a hundred options, it becomes burdensome and our brain shuts down.

In the book *The Paradox of Choice,* Barry Schwartz makes a distinction between "satisficing" and maximizing. Satisficing is when people approach options presented to them with enough energy to make a good-enough decision—no more, no less. Maximizing, on the other hand, requires intense energy to weigh the trade-offs for the best possible decision. When tests were given to people who are extreme maximizers (those who don't stop until they have the best of all possible decisions), their scores put them in the borderline clinical depression range. We all have access to the same information, but spending intense attention on every decision you have to make has been shown to be not healthy.

To make matters more complicated, we tend to spend more time and energy trying to understand the complexities surrounding our personal finances, which leads to information overload, and thus decision fatigue. Instead of making beneficial decisions that would move us forward, we're rendered overwhelmed with options and fail to make a decision. In these situations, progress suffers.

Today, we have endless choices, but we are not always happier for it. With the abundance of choices, we inadvertently place an expectation that the choice we make needs to be perfect. Real life is rarely perfect, though, and when we spend an intense amount of energy making every decision, we risk being disappointed (and depressed) in the end—and decision fatigue becomes chronic.

ARCHITECTING IRRATIONALITY

In their book, *Nudge*, authors Richard Thaler and Cass Sunstein differentiated "Econs" from humans:

> Econs are efficient calculators imagined in economic theory, able to weigh multiple options, forecast all the

consequences of each, and choose rationally. The latter are ordinary people, who...fall short of homo economicus. Humans operate by rules of thumb that often lead them astray. They are too prone to generalize biased in favor of the status quo.

We are not econs. We are human. We have emotions and biases. When economists and marketers build models, they're linear and neat, based on human beings who consistently act in their best interest. When the price goes down, for example, people react by buying more, and that is expressed as a straight line in a graph. Unfortunately, humans and markets don't act in such clean, linear lines. We are biased, irrational, and full of flawed mental models.

Limiting choices doesn't solve our problems completely. Our ability to make sound decisions also depends on our current frame of mind. Marketers spend a lot of money trying to get you to make a decision in what is called a "hot state," which is to say an impulsive or urgent one. A cold state, on the other hand, is when your emotions are in check and you're able to think rationally. In a cold state, you consider whether a purchase or a decision is wise or necessary. A hot state is like grocery shopping when you're hungry; you're more likely to buy items you normally wouldn't buy—think junk food—because those hunger pangs are taking over and everything in that moment sounds delicious. When it comes to investing, the hot state is a "financial expert" from the media. He or she is trying to engage all of your senses, using certain phrases and flashy gimmicks in order to rile up your emotions enough to make brash and impulsive decisions.

I'm pretty sure you can figure out which the preferred state is. (Hint: don't listen to Jim Cramer right before making a big financial decision.)

Making a choice in the wrong state can be as damaging as trying to make a choice out of a sea of options. You aren't paralyzed, per se, but you aren't thinking either—your frame of mind matters.

The overconfidence bias is another landmine to be aware of. I've seen this illustrated at conferences I attend. Inevitably the speaker will ask the members of the audience to raise their hands if they think they are a better-than-average driver. Far more than 50 percent of the audience raises their hands. Logically, these people can't all be better than average, and yet most people think they are.

Side note: I am a terrible driver. I can't see out of my left eye—and even *I* wanted to raise my hand as an "above average" driver.

Thaler, who is also a professor at University of Chicago Booth School of Business, conducted a study in his class of graduate students and asked them to pick which decile they thought they'd be in at the end of the school year—the top 10 percent, the middle 30 percent, and so on. Logically, if the students had a good grasp of their capabilities, the results should be a nice bell curve or should at least add up to 100 percent. In practice, however, *more than 50 percent of students thought they'd be in the top 10 percent*, and almost no one thought they'd be in the bottom half of the class. Mathematically, that can't happen, yet it often happens in these kinds of studies; humans are prone to overconfidence. Unfortunately, this same overconfidence often transfers to topics that people aren't professionals in (like finances!), and—not surprisingly—the consequences can be problematic.

Marketers use the anchoring effect all the time. When you go to Nordstrom, for example, you'll see $400 suits for men. They also sell $2,000 suits, not because they think they're going to sell a lot of them, but because the $400 suits look like a steal once they've anchored you to a $2,000 suit.

This kind of choice architecture is why you're always lost in Las Vegas casinos. The buildings are designed to be winding and confusing so you're forced to walk by slot machines and tables regardless of where you're heading. Casinos don't display clocks or windows, either—also done on purpose. They don't want you to leave; they want you to stay and spend (i.e., lose) your money gambling.

Given all of this, it's important to understand the principles of choice architecture, that the choices you're presented with are designed in a certain way to get you to act a certain way. Think back to the financial "gurus" on television or in print: they want to make it seem like you're gaining something from them so you keep returning to watch their advertisements.

FIGHTING BACK

Making quality choices is as much about the options as it is about the process. Be aware of the biases and the way marketers use those biases to constrain our choices. Most of all, let those hot-state, "urgent" choices pass you by.

When tempted to make decisions in a hot state, channel the respected warrior and Trojan War hero, Ulysses. When he and his men encountered the sirens on their journey home to Ithaca, Ulysses told his crew to fill their ears with beeswax so they could continue rowing the ship without being seduced by the sirens' song. Since Ulysses was curious to hear what the sirens would sing to him, he ordered his men to tie him tightly to the mast of their ship, so no matter what he heard or how he pleaded, he couldn't act on the sirens' temptations.

Regardless what is going on in the market or how crazy it seems, be Ulysses during those hot states—hold yourself back.

Sometimes it's easier to change your environment than your choices. If you want to eat healthier, remove all the Milk Duds (my favorite) from your house and fill the fridge with lean protein, fruits, and vegetables. When junk food isn't a readily available option, you won't eat it! There are other tips as well. When shopping for groceries, for example, if you only shop the perimeter and never go down the center aisles, you'll limit your choices to the healthiest options, again limiting yourself from sugary and processed foods.

Most of all, though, learn to "satisfice." If it's not massively important to your life, it's not worth the extra energy drain to make an ideal choice. "Good enough" *is* good enough for most decisions. It's better to move forward with a less-than-ideal choice in noncritical areas of your life than to become paralyzed with indecision, or exhausted with too much information.

When you successfully do this, you'll be primed to focus on the decisions that have a much larger impact on your life, which will thus result in more beneficial choices.

THE BEST SYSTEM FOR THE CHOICE

In *Thinking, Fast and Slow,* author Daniel Kahneman talks about the two ways the brain makes decisions as system one and system two. System one is automatic, and system two is reflective. For system one, a good example is walking by someone and knowing in the space of a second that they're upset. If someone asks you what two plus two is, you'll quickly answer four without thinking about it. When a bear walks into your office, you get out of your office! (Why would a bear be in an office? I have no idea, but I digress.) These are all system-one thinking.

System-two thinking, on the other hand, is much slower and requires deliberation. If I asked you what twenty-eight times thirty-four is, you could figure it out, but you'd probably need some extra time to do so. It's a learned process, not a natural one.

System-one decisions, the snap decisions, are subject to all the biases we've just pointed out. They might not require as much energy to make, but because of our biases, they can get you in quite a bit of trouble. On important decisions (and pricey ones), it's better to apply system-two thinking. Sit back, be reflective and deliberate, and weigh the pros and cons. Work slowly. Your final answer will be better. For smaller decisions, it's often worth making good-enough choices to save the mental energy for the big stuff.

As the CEO of your life, spend your energy on decisions that have the highest impact. Steve Jobs (black turtle neck) and Mark Zuckerberg (gray shirt) understood how choices work in this way. Jobs didn't spend hours picking out clothes every morning; he made more meaningful decisions that made Apple one of the most successful companies in the world. The same can be said for Zuckerberg and the social media king, Facebook. Since we all only have so much energy to spend on decisions before getting fatigued, how you spend it matters.

Steven Pressfield, in *The War of Art,* writes about resistance, the force we all have fighting to keep us from being our best self. Because of this, the tendency is to spend our time on easy decisions that don't matter. Big decisions are hard and require a lot of deep thinking; people put off estate planning for years *because* it's a hard conversation, overwhelming, and a bit over their heads. They let their portfolios go without thinking about how they'd react to different markets, and they consequently leave themselves financially exposed.

GOOD DECISIONS REQUIRE GOOD OPTIONS

How do you make good decisions in the end? Start with getting a small set of good options.

As we've learned from the jam study, more options do not

mean better choices. If your surgeon gave you a choice between nine surgeries with minor variations, you'd feel overwhelmed and unable to distinguish what is best for you among all the slight differences. If she contrasts an invasive and a noninvasive option with pros and cons, on the other hand, there's enough distinction between the options to let you make an informed choice.

The same argument can be made when you hire professional advisors. Many people hire multiple financial consultants, and then they find it challenging to figure out who to listen to because each consultant offers different advice. It's also true of how you structure your life. When I talk to people about their businesses, I tell them not to set fifty goals for the year, but instead to set three.

Set three, hit three.

If it's not a major decision, "satisfice." It's not worth the effort to dig through to an ideal decision. But if it is a major decision, especially one that has a profound impact, narrow down your list of options and apply system-two thinking. When faced with a tough decision, many people look for every possible option, but this is an endless distraction that hurts your ability to decide. Once you have a small group of options, ideally no more than three, spend the time to compare and contrast the choices before making your final decision.

The reason you want to manage information overload and decision fatigue is so that you can *become the CEO of your life.*

In the next chapter, we turn our attention to doing just that, with a focus on values: the ideals that drive how we think about important decisions—financial *and* otherwise.

CHAPTER THREE

BECOME THE CEO

It's time to take charge and become the CEO of your life. In my experience, most people want to feel empowered to focus on where they want their family, business, and life to go. They want to focus on their vision of the future.

Unfortunately, most people don't properly act like the CEO, because they're overwhelmed.

The reason for managing information overload and decision fatigue is so you can regain control of your life. I think it's safe to say that most people want to be in control of where their future is headed. So, what does a CEO do? A CEO identifies core values—whether for a company or for a family. Core values are the company's or family's *why*—their North Star; the reason behind why they make the decisions they make.

A company like Zappos has a different *why* than the Ritz Carlton, for example, set forth by the CEO. Each company's core values dictate the way they operate and how they make decisions, and it's no different when it comes to families. We have family CEOs who say, "What's important to me is giving to others." That's a completely different decision and financial plan than the family CEO who says, "What's most important to me is enjoying my life with my kids and grandkids." Neither of these is wrong; they're just a different set of values, which means they come with a different way to make decisions.

Being the CEO means defining that vision, understanding your core values, and then sharing them with those important to you. Once you do that, you can identify short- and long-term goals that align with those values.

Most people are the CEO and the CFO in their life, but they require fundamentally different mindsets. A big part of the reason why so many family CEOs (which is you) are overwhelmed is because they try to take on both roles.

CORE VALUES AND GOALS

It's critical to understand the difference between a core value and a goal. Personally, my core values are excellence, continuous improvement, and fun. For me, the enemy of great is good; I'm always looking to do better; and if I'm not having fun, perhaps I shouldn't be doing what I'm doing. I apply these values to everything I do, including my business.

My values don't change by the business. They are always excellence, continuous improvement, and fun. The North Star doesn't move. The idea here is that no matter what the business is, core values would not change. If I were to become a plumber, these would still be my core values. I would want to be the best plumber, I would want to learn to get better, and I would want to have fun while cleaning your toilet. (I'd be the happiest plumber you'd ever met!) This is the lens I view through to make *all* of my decisions—in business, with my family, and through life.

If I won the lottery, I'd likely give the money away because it wouldn't align with my core values. I'd rather work hard and earn something rather than it be handed to me. That's where the fun and enjoyment comes in for me, knowing I worked until my fingers bled to achieve my goals. Everyone is different. Some people think giving money away is crazy. There's no right or wrong answer here. It's all about what's most important to you.

Once you know your values, they shouldn't change. They should permeate everything you do. Your goals, on the other hand, can change. The goal is the output. The value or vision is the lens through which we decide what goals to set.

Some clients can't initially articulate what their core values are, so that's the first thing we figure out together. Once established, when they try to make future decisions that aren't in line with their core values, I can advise them appropriately.

THE VALUE CARDS EXERCISE

It's the CEO's job to set the destination based on values.

In one of the first meetings I have with new clients, we start with an important game. I open up a new deck of "value cards" from a company called Think2Perform, and I explain the purpose. The exercise provides an interactive way to define what clients value most, which later helps us guide them in their decision-making process. It's fun to see the client loosen up a bit since most people don't find talking about their finances that fun or exciting.

Each deck has forty-nine cards, and each card has a different value written on it with a brief description. Values include autonomy, challenges, competence, decisiveness, education, fairness, family, happiness, integrity, loyalty, money, power, religion, service, stability, wealth, work, and so on. The goal is for the client to end up with five cards that are the most important to them.

There are many ways to end up with five final cards (values), but my favorite is to lay out the first five from the deck in a row on a table. Let's say the cards are adventure, ethics, play, change, and security. Handing the rest of the deck to the client, I'd instruct her to take the next card from the top and decide whether the value on that card is greater than one of the five on the table. If so, the client puts that value over the card that is of lesser importance. Say the client's card was wealth, which is more important to her than adventure. She'd place the wealth card over the adventure card. If the client gets to a value card that is less important than the five on the table, she simply discards it. The client continues until the entire deck is gone and she is left with her five most important values.

I ask clients at that point to choose three of their five, which sometimes proves to be challenging. Five values are usually good, but if they can get it down to three, it's much easier to help guide them through decision-making down the line. I love starting our relationship with this exercise because it allows them to think differently about their choices. If my three core values are health, family, and fun, for example, and I'm working my tail off for seventy hours a week, eating fast food because it's convenient, and drinking several beers each day to cope with the stress, clearly there's a disconnect. It's easy to see that lifestyle doesn't match my values.

When I sit down with a client and she tells me she's going to keep working until she's seventy years old so she can accumulate more money, but I know her values are health, family, and fun, that's a red flag. A lot of people spend the first part of their life trading their health for wealth, and then later spend all their wealth trying to get their health back—and that's what we spend our life doing: trading one thing for another. Often you're trading life (time) for financial wealth, so there will be limits to how much you have of each depending on how you choose to trade.

It becomes much easier to make decisions when you use values as your guide.

WHAT DOES A CFO DO?

A CFO is the expert in *you*, the CEO. If you've done the work to identify your values and your goals, you've established your *what* and your *why*. The CFO's job is to figure out *how* to make those happen. Throughout all this, he becomes an expert in *you*. The CFO creates a strategy, explains it, and highlights the implications so the CEO can stay informed and make sound decisions down the line when needed.

As the expert in you, a big part of a CFO's job is to be a

relevance filter. We live in an age of information, but as we know, more information isn't always the answer. If it was, we'd all be billionaires with six-pack abs. Sometimes the right information at the right time matters far more, because then you can *act* on what's more significant. The CFO filters out all the noise surrounding your goals and only presents information that matters. Your CFO will tell you as much or as little as you want to know about the details that matter to *you*—the strategy, execution, and path are taken care of. The CFO keeps the minutiae off the CEO's plate and keeps information overload, decision fatigue, and any other distractions at bay.

The relationship between the CEO and the CFO isn't about money management; it's about better decision-making. Successful CFOs thus allow CEOs to focus on other, more important things—whether that's spending more time with family, running a business, traveling the world, and so on. A CFO gives them the freedom to pursue what they want.

The value of the CFO is that he allows you to actually *be the CEO*.

THE METHOD AND THE GOAL

Many clients come in with a method in mind, as opposed to a goal. This is where we want to shift their thinking into focusing on the goal (CEO's responsibility) so we can focus on the method (CFO's responsibility).

For example, a client walks in and tells us she wants to grow her portfolio to $X amount (the amount doesn't matter).

"Okay, Sandra," I'll say. "Why do you want to grow your portfolio to that amount? So that you can..."

"So that I can retire and not have to work anymore."

This is one of the most common answers, but it is not the end goal. People want to retire so that they could do something, so I prod again.

"So that you can..."

"So that I can buy a lake house so my grandkids can come every summer."

There we go—that's the CEO's goal. The CFO handles the method once the CEO establishes the goal. *I want X so that I can do Y*. The phrase, "So that I can..." translates the method to a goal. It's much easier to put things in place to achieve the goal of a lake house than the limited methods of growing a portfolio to an arbitrary amount.

Toyota's manufacturing department does a similar process

to get to the bottom of issues by using the "Five Whys." When an issue pops up, they ask why to get to the heart of the matter, which usually takes five times. I do the same thing with "So that you can..." It pushes my clients from the method (some arbitrary number) to the goal (what they really want).

People confuse method and goal all the time, and the information overload doesn't help. When someone is seeking an insurance policy and I ask them why, if the first thing that pops out of their mouth is, "Well, I read on Google..."—that's information overload.

Having a CFO means you have someone who knows what you want, and then finds the right formulas at the right times to get you what you want. You don't have to wade through the sea of generic information to find something useful you can use. You can focus on being the CEO of your life.

WHO NEEDS A CFO?

Successful CEOs are typically good at delegating, because they know they only have twenty-four hours in a day. They spend their time on the highest-value decisions and activities, the things they enjoy, are really good at, or matter the most, and they delegate the rest to others.

Some people are better delegators than others, some

would rather learn and do everything themselves, and some have a hard time trusting others. These people sometimes have a hard time being CEOs. There is a lot in life you *can* do yourself, if you're willing to spend enough time and mental energy on it—not to mention willing to accept that you won't do it as well as an expert. The trade-offs are real, though, and information overload, decision fatigue, and limited time apply to everyone.

There are a lot of things in life that need to be done. The question is, *which ones truly need to be done by you?* Which set of worries can you let someone else handle?

The more successful you are, the more complex your situation (i.e., life) tends to become. While most people can handle opening a savings account and contributing a certain amount a month from their first job, at a certain point of success, the decisions around finances (and beyond) become more challenging with more moving parts that need to be integrated.

When you reach that point as your own CEO, you have to delegate to others or it doesn't get done. As the *Harvard Business Review* says, you go from a "crisis of delegation" to a "crisis of collaboration." It's not just how and when to delegate; it's how all of the many decisions and professionals start working together. At that point, it's like a pond filled with lily pads on the surface; you drop a rock (make a decision) in the pond, and all of the lily pads (the other parts of your life) move.

If you're making big decisions, suddenly every decision matters. It's going to impact your estate plan, your insurance, your taxes, and the rest of the lily pads in the pond. If you're starting to have to deal with those types of decisions, a CFO becomes essential because the complexity is now growing exponentially. It's not about getting the best in each silo anymore; it's about making sure all your silos are working together toward your goals together. You don't want a major decision to benefit one silo, but then destroy another.

When you build a house, you want to hire a good general contractor who can work with the fifty or sixty specialists necessary to build your house. Unless you have deep knowledge of contracting, you're not going to want to spend your time finding and supervising all those people. Even if you did, if you don't know that the plumbing needs to go down before the electrical, you could end up with a cascading series of mistakes—a crisis of integration. It will be an expensive mistake that could have been avoided.

Typically, clients don't want to build the house; they want to own the house, weigh in on the design decisions with the architect for the final product, and then have it built by professionals. In other words, do you want to know what time it is, or do you want to spend your life learning how the watch is made?

TRUST

One of the biggest challenges with hiring someone in your life to be the CFO is trust. This is a natural part of human nature, especially among those who worked their tails off to achieve success. Unsurprisingly, people find it difficult to trust someone else with this level of responsibility.

People struggle with trusting someone to be in this middle position, which is funny because they're already trusting multiple individuals working in silos. What we're talking about is having somebody who helps all these individuals work together, and if you don't have that person, then it's you. Like the lily pad analogy, one big change you didn't plan for can make the whole pond move in ways that can cost you immense amounts of money, time, and opportunity. It's not a position to fill with just anyone—you have to look for someone who knows more than you and who can spend their time and human capital on it.

Trying to do both the CEO role and the CFO role does not result in executing either one well, or sometimes at all. It's why clients come into my office without a clear understanding of their values and goals. They're so bogged down in the small details that they can't make the kind of critical CEO decisions they need to be making.

It's important to understand, however, that just as in any other relationship, real trust takes time to build. The longer you stay with a single CFO, the more you'll trust them and the more they will understand you. In the beginning, as Ronald Reagan said, "Trust but verify." While it's great to have this trusted advisor, it's important that they're accountable to the financial parameters that you've established.

Building trust with your CFO is like building trust with your doctor. You want to see if they'll ask good questions about you. You want to see what they recommend, listen to which questions they ask, and see how they talk to you. The best professional is going to be the one who takes the time to listen and to get to know what you need.

Work with someone who is going to ask about your core values. Are you going to be comfortable exchanging cell phone numbers with this person? Are you going to be comfortable telling them everything that's important to your life and your family? Are you going to be comfortable with this person knowing everything about you? If not, don't hire them.

Before you hire someone, have your potential CFO explain

their process to you in detail. What is their process for learning and understanding everything about you and your family? How do they build a plan for getting the details done? And lastly, how do they know you're on track? This person needs to be able to clearly articulate and identify how these things will be done and, as we will see in the following chapters, to act as your advocate, catalyst, integrator.

PART

II

THE ROLES

CHAPTER FOUR

THE ADVOCATE

ad·vo·cate
/'advəkət/
noun

1. a person who publicly supports or recommends a particular cause or policy. Synonyms: supporter, champion, proposer, counsel, defender.

People read and watch self-help financial gurus, expecting to receive personal, earth-shattering advice. While some of the advice might seem relevant, you have to ask yourself if it's pertinent to you and your specific situation. Don't forget what the motivation behind sharing such information is: to get you to keep watching.

The truth is, nobody knows what's going to happen in the

markets. If there are ten thousand financial gurus, and all of them made random predictions, statistically speaking a small number of them will be right thirty times in a row. This is not because they're geniuses, but because that's how statistics work. If you had that many people flipping coins, you'd get some people landing tails thirty times in a row too. Furthermore, as we've discussed in chapter 1, the media wants you to keep reading and watching, so everything they put out is designed to keep you coming back rather than giving you a beneficial answer.

Remember my warning about media sources sharing "secrets"? If somebody knows a secret in the financial world, the only way they can make money is if they don't tell anybody, so why would they share it? These news sources are trying to make money off you. If financial news stations can make something sound more urgent than it is, they will. They're only sharing the lower part of the DIKW triangle: data and information. They'll make something sound new and different, even if it isn't. Now, the media is not malicious; I don't think they're going out of their way to not solve your problems. But by design, they can't solve your problems, because they don't know anything about you, because there's no application.

Quality advice is based on principles. Just as important, it's also based on your individual situation. With your values and goals in mind, and with the financial expertise within the industry, a personal CFO is your advocate, putting a solid strategy in place.

A solid strategy shouldn't change often, if at all. Tactics, on the other hand, change constantly, and that's why these self-proclaimed "financial gurus" focus on tactics to keep you coming back for more.

If your goal doesn't change, the plan doesn't change.

Even when these gurus say things worth listening to—it happens on occasion—they're only dealing out content on the data and information level. There's no way of knowing what, if anything, they say actually applies to you and your family. Without a clear idea of your values and your long-term goals, you're drowning in information without any useful direction.

While you are enjoying your life traveling, spending time with grandkids, or volunteering for worthy causes, the CFO keeps tabs and works in the background on your behalf, advocating for you and making sure things are on track for you to reach your goals.

EVERY PROBLEM LOOKS LIKE A NAIL

Don't ask a barber if you need a haircut.

—PROVERB

We need to understand capabilities and the lens in which people view problems. If you go to an Audi dealership, they're going to try to sell you an Audi. They're not doing anything wrong; you read the sign on the door before you walked in.

A disability insurance or life insurance salesperson will do the same thing. It doesn't mean she is bad at the job—often these salespeople are great at what they do. When all you have is a hammer, though, every problem looks like a nail. The salesperson can't tell you whether or not you should be having the conversation in the first place. If you go to someone who specializes in surgery, that's going to be his primary method of helping you. His lens is, "How can I solve your problem with the things that I'm good at? What's my toolbox?" Which makes sense; you're going to a conduit, essentially. You're going to somebody who offers a specific solution, so the impression is that you're looking to buy that. Their job is to sell you that solution.

A few years back, I visited a sports surgeon to talk about issues I had with my shoulder. He recommended a surgery where he would break the joint, put my shoulder in a cast, and allow it to heal over several months. He told me it "would probably help." Well, I wasn't willing to go through that kind of pain and expense for a "probably," so I visited a physical therapist to see if he could help. He offered an alternative approach that helped significantly. After about a month, the issues completely went away.

I'm not angry at the surgeon for trying to solve problems presented to him with surgery. That's what surgeons do. I was happy to find a solution that didn't involve invasive surgery. It's important to realize how often good people are driven by their specialties more than your needs. Always consider that the unique lens in which people view your problem drives how they view solving your problem.

CONDUIT VERSUS THINKING PARTNER

A conduit is a person or thing that gets you the commodity you want without much extra thought or consideration. You want something? No problem! It's done. In real estate, realtors get a bad name because they're often seen as unnecessary conduits. They show you a house they have limited knowledge on, encourage you to purchase, and they go make an offer on your behalf. If escrow is successful, congratulations! You have a house, but you also pay the realtor commission when you could have bought that house through a service online and saved the money that went to the realtor for doing minimal work. You're paying someone a lot of money for access.

If all you're looking for is somebody who's going to place the order, technology has likely solved that problem, and you can find that service for free online. Instead, look for a thinking partner who will make sure your actions match up with your real goals, and who will get you to the end you're looking for. You're looking for someone who can see past your blind spots and can implement and execute what you *really* need, not just what you want.

THE BIG PICTURE

The CFO's job is to look at you and your current state of affairs with a wide-lens view. He knows and understands your goals and your values, and he's able to find the best methods to achieve them *for your situation*. The CFO's job is to get you from point A to point B in the best way possible. He is *your* advocate. If that means finding experts to help assist with the method, that's what he'll do. The CFO takes the mental load off the CEO and seeks experts out, vets them, and then folds them into the big picture.

This advocate role is missing in most relationships, which can lead to problems. You need to have someone who has a holistic view of your situation; otherwise, you'll be pushed around from one expert to another. If you bring a question about inheriting a business to your tax professional, if she doesn't know the answer, she'll just send you to another professional. She'll say, "That's not my job." If the question or issue at hand doesn't have a direct correlation with their expertise or array of services, they'll point you to someone else (with no guarantee that the next person will know the answer, either). Unlike a CFO, they don't want to spend the time or energy on the whole you; they're only focused on their limited knowledge and array of services.

Picture the CFO wearing a VELCRO® suit where all your values, goals, and problems stick, and he is responsible for everything. Specialists, on the other hand, through no fault of their own, wear Teflon® suits—nothing sticks to them. The Velcro suit means that when you call, no matter what the problem is, the CFO will help you. Regardless of the issue, your personal CFO will find and vet the expert needed and make sure you get the right answer in a timely fashion.

Your CFO is your biggest advocate, and that means she focuses on the right people and methods to help achieve your goals. The CFO never says, "That's not my job."

GREASING THE WHEELS

As your advocate, your CFO can help in situations you come in contact with every day. Let's take buying a car as an example. When it comes time to buy a car, we all enjoy test-driving cars, but the rest of the car-buying experience is painful. No one likes to sit at a dealership for six hours trying to negotiate a deal.

A client of mine, Vicki (not her real name), walked into my office and said, "I need to buy a new car, but I hate the process." I told her I would be happy to assist.

Vicki told me her price range, what she wanted in a car (her must-haves), and what she could do without. She already had an idea of which car she wanted. I talked Vicki through any questions and made sure I understood her parameters. I then told her to go to the dealership and tell a salesman which car she wanted, hand them my business card, and tell them, "My CFO will be in touch with you."

It was easy for me to conduct the transaction over the phone. I told the dealer that I was interviewing three different dealerships and I needed their best and final offer. I told them that Vicki liked them and that she would love to work with them, but that it's very much about price, and I instructed them to let me know the price by the end of the day.

This way, no one's stuck in the dealership for six hours, and they have no way of trying to grind me down with the process, because I'm not physically there. I can also handle the process better because I don't have any emotions in it. It's a hardline discussion, and I set the right expectations with the salesperson from the get-go. Once the deal between the dealer and I was final, I told Vicki to go in, sign, and pick up the keys the next day. I help clients with this not because we save them so much money (although we do); more importantly, I can handle things like this with very little energy on my part and save my clients from the headache of the entire scenario.

It's easy for a CFO to talk to people like dealers because they understand the language and therefore a client doesn't get jerked around. It's the effect of "call my attorney," only you're dealing with the one person who handles your attorney, your CPA, your insurance guy, and so on.

A client might save a few thousand dollars, but the real advantage of a CFO is the client doesn't have to deal with things like negotiating at a dealership for hours on end. People are more excited to not have to handle negotiating deals or dealing with paperwork than they are when they save money during the process.

LET FREEDOM RING

When you're not worried about details, you have the freedom to live your life. The CFO provides this freedom. Your complexity is managed so you can make better decisions—financial and otherwise. Your CFO has set the course, and you'll get to your destination without the stress.

Anything your CFO can handle is one less thing you have to handle. You have the freedom to focus on what you need to focus on, knowing that someone else is taking great care of you and your family. It goes back to the trade-off concept. How much of your life do you want to be trading? Time is your one nonrenewable resource.

Many people are afraid to pursue what they care most about, because they worry they'll fail or they won't have enough money. Your CFO is in your corner to encourage, push, and help you plan so there's enough money and enough contingency plans to help you arrive at your big goals.

We've all made big mistakes in our lives. What if you had someone in your corner to use as a sounding board? Would you have made the same mistakes? Successful people, like everyone else, have blind spots, which is to be expected. We cannot all be experts in everything. Putting pieces together into a coherent whole is about asking good questions. Successful people often don't want someone to tell them the answer; they want help getting *to* the right answer. That's part of the CFO's job, to be that sounding board, because a CFO has financial expertise they don't. Having someone who knows when to be a sounding board and when to be prescriptive means you have a good CFO.

THE CONSIGLIERE

When I think of a personal CFO as an advocate, I think of *The Godfather* and the consigliere.

In *The Godfather*, the consigliere is the right-hand man to the Mafia boss. He is his advisor, the person who knows everything there is about the family, and one of the few allowed to question the boss. He'd be the go-between for the boss and the people in the family or business if one was needed, and anything the boss asked him to handle, he'd handle. He wouldn't say, "That's not my job."

Your CFO should be your consigliere. For a CFO to do what he needs to do well, he needs to be able to think like the family, and yet apply his more than ten thousand hours of expertise in finances directly to your situation. He needs to be able to challenge you to think about your best interests and values before acting, and be ready and prepared to handle anything that is thrown at him. The consigliere is a partner sitting at the table, a thinking partner who can be trusted to get things done. A personal CFO is trusted with the big picture and should both advise and execute.

CHAPTER FIVE

THE CATALYST

cat·a·lyst
/ˈkad(ə)ləst/
noun

1. A person who quickly causes change or action. Synonyms:
impetus, motivator, stimulant, change maker.

The best ideas in the world are worthless without execution.

Your CFO's job is to be a catalyst, the means by which progress or change is sped up. She is tasked to get you from point A to B in a stable, sustainable way, and that means handling a large percentage of the process seamlessly. Even so, there is inevitably a portion that requires the CEO's involvement, but that's when the CFO becomes your accountability partner to make sure you are on track to reach your goals.

If you want to get in shape, you need to go to the gym. If you want to lose weight, you have to burn more calories than you consume. There's no information shortage when it comes to fitness; you know what you need to do. All too often, however, we don't put the work in to reach our fitness goals, especially when we try to do it on our own. There are plenty of studies that show a fitness partner increases your chances of reaching fitness goals because you're more likely to follow through. This person keeps you accountable. They're a catalyst. That's why hiring a personal trainer makes such a huge difference.

The CFO is a catalyst for complex interdependent systems. It's his job to minimize the number of things you have to deal with and to make them happen, but you'll need to be involved on a high level. If you've hired a general contractor to build your house, you'd want to pick out the faucets, but you wouldn't want to install the floors.

Similarly, as the CEO you need to decide on the direction you're going. There are decisions you'll have to make along the way, but the implementation and the method are things that are handled by the team of people who ultimately work for you, and the CFO is the catalyst who will make it happen in the best possible way. He will also hold your feet to the fire to do the things that only you can do.

Estate planning is a great example; people hate it, but they know they need to do it. It's not hard, but people don't like it because no one likes to talk about dying. Who wants to make an appointment to talk about their death? It's the CFO's responsibility to talk through all the implications and make sure you have all the information necessary to make the best possible decision.

When we talked about information overload in chapter 1, we talked about how after any big decision, there are two steps: application and integration. How do we apply the decision to the estate plan so that it's executed well? Then, how does that decision affect all the other silos (tax, insurance, investments, etc.)? How can we work with the whole financial situation given this one change that affects the rest for maximum benefit across the board?

One of the best parts of having a catalyst is how much more they accomplish on your behalf. A catalyst speeds up your rate of change, or gets you more progress faster than you could accomplish by yourself. Often a financial advisor tries to hand too much work to the CEO, which is a mistake. You're the CEO, and the CFO works for you. A good CFO will take the work off your plate when it comes to execution. When it comes to decisions, however, you're the CEO. The buck stops with you.

The CFO guides. The CEO decides.

Most people have a decent understanding of what should be happening in their financial lives, but they're not acting on that understanding. Why is that? The sheer number of things to do feels overwhelming. When you hire a CFO, you're hiring someone who not only will be your thinking partner and advocate, but will take a huge portion of the tasks off your plate.

MANAGING EXPECTATIONS

Part of the CFO's job is to manage your expectations. If you want to accomplish 113 financial things in the next three months, your CFO will bring you back down to earth and tell you that's not realistic. He will then help bring those goals down to achievable next steps that will have the biggest impact.

Happiness = outcomes – expectations

Happiness boils down to outcomes minus the expectations. Even with the best possible outcome in the world, if your expectations are too high, you won't be all that happy. Sometimes setting expectations is challenging, but the result is much better than setting you up for disappointment, and a good CFO knows this.

Take opinions on movies, for example. I love watching movies; it's one of my favorite things to do. If you tell me a particular movie was the best thing you've ever seen, my expectations of it will be extremely high—which then makes it impossible for me to be happy with the movie. Anything other than mind-blowing brilliance becomes a disappointment. On the opposite side of the spectrum, when someone tells me a movie is the worst movie they've ever seen and they wish they could get their two hours back, I'll likely be thrilled with it upon seeing it myself. My expectations were so low walking into the movie that anything average makes me happy.

If your boss tells you you're going to get a $1,000,000 bonus in January, you'd be beyond thrilled and immediately share the news with your spouse. It doesn't stop there, though. You'd likely start mental accounting, fantasizing about what you would do with the bonus money. You might even make a list of things to buy, trips to go on, and so on. Your lifestyle balloons based on what you *think may be coming.*

Then, on December 31, your boss informs you that, actually, your bonus is only going to be $50,000. Now you're upset. If you bought a car in anticipation of the bigger bonus, you're now returning it. If you hired a maid, you're putting her on notice. You might be so angry with your boss that you might even be looking for another job.

If, however, she'd come to you at the beginning of the year and told you that your bonus would be nothing, and then surprised you in December with $50,000, you'd be over the moon! Despite receiving the same amount in each scenario, the emotional impact on you would have been drastically different based on your expectations.

CLEAR DECISION-MAKING

I would not give a fig for the simplicity this side of complexity, but I would give my life for the simplicity on the other side of complexity.

—OLIVER WENDELL HOLMES

In a world where we're drowning in complex information, finding clarity isn't easy.

When you're tackling a new challenge, especially in the area of finance, the more you learn, the more complicated the terrain gets, and it will stay that complicated for a long, long time.

Your CFO is there to help you navigate the complex terrain in a simple, straightforward way. It's her job to make the line straighten out again. That's getting to the other side of complexity. Complexity is often intimidating, and some people try to avoid it. Don't; it won't do you any good. Acknowledge the complexity, and seek help. Treating a complex topic as if it were simple means inevitably getting caught by what you don't know. The other side of complexity, however, is knowing the subject so well that it can be explained simply. The other side of complexity is about knowledge and wisdom—which take a lot of learning to get there.

If you ever want to know if someone knows their topic, whether that topic is teaching, entrepreneurship, the law, or anything else, ask them to explain it to you in a simple metaphor or story. It takes a whole different level of expertise to explain it to a fourth grader; that's why Neil deGrasse Tyson is so popular. He can explain astrophysics in terms anyone can understand.

Your CFO should be able to explain complex financial tools in terms you can understand. She should be able to present the decisions that need to be made simply, in a context that makes it relevant to your situation, so you can decide easily between limited choices. As the catalyst, that's a key part of what she does, and advanced knowledge is critical.

CHAPTER SIX

THE INTEGRATOR

in·te·gra·tor
/ ˈin(t)əˌɡrādər/
noun

1. a person or thing that integrates, bringing together or incorporating (parts) into a whole. Synonyms: assimilator, blender, orchestrator, organizer.

The more success you achieve, the more complex your finances become. As the decisions you make get more important, every part of your financial life starts to have its own expert. It gets to the level where you aren't comfortable making the decisions anymore.

Then, as you get even more successful and the system grows even more complex, even having professionals to help you isn't as effective. Your financial life gets to the point where you don't know how to apply the advice that one professional gives you in a way that doesn't negatively affect the advice that other professionals gave you. You can't integrate it anymore.

In chemistry, there's a distinction between adhesion and cohesion. Cohesion is when similar things hold together, like the molecules of water holding on to one another for surface tension. Adhesion is when different things cling to one another; this is why glue is called an adhesive, since it bonds different things together. Adhesion is much harder than cohesion. The reason that finances become difficult is because adhesion is needed; you have different subject matters that need to come together into a plan that makes sense. This would be easy if you had four of the same things, but you don't. There are completely different subjects (tax, estate, investments, insurance, etc.) all coming together, and they need to stick to your goals. The trouble is, all of these areas are like different languages (i.e., like trying to learn Arabic, French, Latin, and Japanese all at once). Even if you could learn them all, trying to integrate the ideas in each and get each to work together is challenging, even for professionals. A CFO specializes in integration, the tricky adhesion of all the different areas into a single whole that works the way you need it to work.

BUILDING A HOUSE

If you want to build a house, without a general contractor, you won't know how to pour your foundation, do pipes or electrical, or get the right people to work together in the right order. Mistakes can cost you major money if you don't know what you're doing.

This dynamic is complicated by the fact that individual professionals aren't going to take the time to work together if they don't have to. The electrician isn't going out of his way to ask about the roofer. He doesn't need to. It's also impossible to build a house with only one subcontractor; even if a plumber was willing to lay your floorboards, you wouldn't want him to. That's why you need a general contractor; having the raw materials stacked up on a lot doesn't mean you have a house. Architecture plans *and* someone who knows how to put everything together are both critical to the process.

If you ask a roofer about the house, all of his advice is going to center around the roof. It might touch on the supports for the roof, but it won't include any of the other hundred things you need for a successful house. He just doesn't have the perspective to see them. Every bit of advice that he'll give you is limited to his specialty, and none of it will help you integrate his specialty into the rest of your financial world.

A CFO solves that problem. Your CFO finds and integrates the right professionals in the right order to follow the plan and goals you've set, and in the end, you have the financial equivalent of a house. It makes sense, and more importantly, it stands up to financial weather.

THE RIGHT TOOLS

The task of integrating your financial house is built on four pillars: integration, application, relevance, and time—which all have risks if you try to handle them yourself. In terms of integration and application, you won't know which professionals to hire—such as whether you need the most expensive estate attorney in the world, or if you're most of the way there already and only need an attorney to confirm the plan.

Think about all that wasted time. Life is short; there's a lot about finances you just don't need to spend the time to learn.

Integration is its own specialty. Financial complexity at a certain level becomes like surgery, just not worth it for your average successful person to learn. Do what you do; let your CFO handle the complexity of integration for you.

MANAGING YOUR TEAM

Every client is different; therefore, every client has different complexities and challenges and will need different sets of professionals to handle them. Your CFO will identify the right people for the job and manage their work for your best results.

Rather than you being the central contact who deals with all the professionals, coordinating the details, and making sure that everything happens, the CFO becomes your one point of contact with an army of professionals below him. It's faster, and you get a better result because your CFO understands how to integrate.

A lot of times with clients there's a resistance to allowing your CFO to build a team because you might like your current insurance guy, or he's your brother-in-law. You can still work with them; they will just need to know that they're part of a greater team, and that they'll be expected to communicate with everyone else to make sure that you—the CEO—get the best outcomes. A CFO will work with whomever you want her to work with, but if someone is difficult, it becomes a matter of asking how much time, energy, and money it is worth spending to continue working with said person.

I have a conversation with my new clients when we're discussing their existing professionals, and I always ask,

"On a scale of zero to ten, how important is working with this person?" Ten means this person has to stay because they're my spouse, and zero is a call for replacement, perhaps because they've committed fraud. There is one rule, however: they cannot rate anyone a seven. A rating of seven doesn't tell me anything. A seven means you're not telling me what you think. If someone rates an employee and says, "Oh, he's an eight or a nine," you'd know exactly what they think. If they say, "He's a five," you know what they think. But if they think he's a seven, you don't know what they think. It's a cop-out.

In my experience, most clients need to reduce the size of their teams overall to run as lean as possible. The right professionals are critical, but when working with a CFO, most clients find that they don't need as many. When we work with professionals on behalf of a client, we also make a point about everyone needing to check their ego at the door. Everyone on the team is smart, or they wouldn't be on the team, but the focus needs to be about what is best for the client—so ask for everyone to collaborate together.

Most people cooperate. If you call them asking for a document the client needs, for example, they'll give it to you, but you have to ask. Integrating means having as much collaboration as possible, making sure everyone understands the big picture and their place in it.

I find that when everyone on the team knows the big picture, suddenly their recommendations start changing. Often the professionals on the team will be nervous to have regular calls together, thinking it will take up so much time. In practice, though, it takes less time overall than phone tag and trying to fix each other's mistakes.

Our clients find it's a big time-saver to have a half-hour call with all of their professionals, with us running the meeting. Rather than the client having to drive all over town and meet with each professional individually, we handle everything over the phone, all together, as a team. The advice that results is a lot better, too, since everyone understands exactly what's going on.

Imagine if you were in any big company and none of the departments talked at all. Sales had no idea what marketing was up to, and operations and manufacturing didn't communicate. The company wouldn't last long, would it? It's the same with finances past a certain point of complexity.

To return to the concepts of adhesion and cohesion, then, it's relatively easy for like things to stick together. Tax and insurance, or estate and investments, won't work together without a lot of integration; that's the advantage of the CFO, because the CFO speaks all their languages and specializes in integration.

PUTTING IT ALL TOGETHER

When you come to your CFO with an issue, you know you'll have a thinking partner to solve it. You'll also know that it will be handled, start to finish, with full integration into the rest of your world. You only have one person to deal with, a single accountable person with a Velcro suit.

As a fulcrum, the CFO deals with all of your professionals for you, providing leverage to finish things better and faster. If you're the general of an army, you don't go to every foot soldier to tell him your orders; you give the order once and trust your team to send it down the line. Having that one point of contact is powerful, not only for you, but as we've discussed, it's also powerful for the professionals working for you.

We find that the majority of our clients come to us when the key person they thought was helping them manage their world isn't. When we start talking to the other members of the team, it turns out there is no team—no one has been working together. The integration role is a critical one. Having a thinking partner who is looking at the big picture while they move the chess pieces for you makes all the difference.

The following chapters cover what a CFO does to effectively take care of you, the CEO, starting with creating a map to establish a solid plan, and continually measuring progress in order to make sure your goals are met.

PART

III

THE PROCESS

CHAPTER SEVEN

CREATE YOUR MAP

When I'm talking to clients, I emphasize two words: *clear* and *shared*. We need a clear, shared understanding of where you are now and where you want to be. If a client says that financial independence means spending more time on the beach, I tell them that there are beaches all over the world and ask them to be more specific. Are we talking Key West? Alaska? Brazil? Padre or La Jolla? "Beach" alone isn't enough. If I call American Airlines and ask to "go somewhere nice," they'll laugh at me. In order to buy an airplane ticket, I need two airport codes to clearly communicate my plans: where I am now, and where I want to go.

When I say "shared," what I mean is that everyone on the team—you (the CEO), your CFO, and everyone on your advisory team—sees the same map. Not an iteration of it, but exactly the same thing. Everyone needs to see your map of where you are now and where you want to go.

> **Where you are now** = Point A (balance sheet, income statement, core values)

> **Where you want to go** = Point B (short-term, midterm, and long-term goals)

Everyone needs to look at the same map of where you want to go. Otherwise, if you just speak in generalities like "Draw me a purple elephant," there will be ten different interpretations of what that looks like—some may be more realistic, others more cartoonish, and everything in between. Everyone needs to be looking at and working on the same *Mona Lisa*.

A VISUAL MAP

While it's possible that a client has a clear idea of where he is and where he wants to go, in all my years of practice I've never seen it; more clarity and depth is always needed. Even the smartest, most prepared people have rarely defined exactly what they want.

Having clearly defined goals is one thing, but a clearly defined starting point is an entire other thing. The starting point is your balance sheet, your financial statements.

Even if they have defined their goals, no one has asked them why—and answering the series of *whys* nearly always changes the original goals. This is why we always start with the core-values exercise, and why mapping is such an important part of the process.

Core values help us guide everything about your map; if your *why* is family, fun, and giving to charity, that's a different journey than one based on excellence, autonomy, and wealth. Even if two people have similar goals, the roads to those goals are often drastically different, given their personal situations. There are multiple options on a road trip from New York to Los Angeles. Would you take the most direct and fastest route, or spend some time exploring small towns along the way? Is it fun for you to hike and fish, or would you rather stay in opulent hotels and order room service?

Once we understand your core values and your general direction, it's a matter of understanding all these other details. There's a big part of this process that's about brainstorming. The rest is about precisely defining what you mean, as simply and visually as possible—which is why we call it mapping. It's important to use diagrams and pictures because it makes your thoughts much clearer and more easily understood by your team.

REPRESENTING CONNECTIONS

map

/map/

noun

1. a diagrammatic representation of an area of land or sea showing physical features, cities, roads, etc.

verb

1. represent (an area) on a map; make a map of.

Map can be used as both a noun and a verb. *A map*, the noun, is a visual representation of terrain, often with a route planned out. It's how we visualize and understand where we are now and where we need to go. *To map*, the verb, is the process of ideation and visualization—it involves brainstorming, and it involves understanding the relationships between ideas.

People will often just list ideas, but that's not how we best process information. It's hard for a successful person to simply write something down in a vertical, list-based format; a list doesn't capture how ideas are interrelated, nor is it a good indicator of what's most important. Part of mapping out a given topic is representing how things are grouped. When we think of certain assets or liabilities, how do we bucket those together? What risk tolerances do we have for different things? Until you literally start drawing circles on a whiteboard, it's difficult to see a clear and shared understanding of a complex topic.

Because of this need to represent relationships between ideas, mapping is a process and can take some time. It shouldn't be done haphazardly, and it's challenging to do fully by yourself. It's helpful to have another lens and someone else asking you questions, forcing you to expand and clarify your thinking. How do you know if you miss something if you're the only one asking the questions? How do you know if you've communicated what you really mean? There's a big difference between the tune going on in your head and the song you're singing out loud.

That's why getting something out of your head and onto paper is a critical part of ideation. Everyone is a little different in the way they absorb information, but interacting with information in an external way helps identify holes and clarify your thoughts. How do these things work together? Your ability to understand the relationship of the moving parts with the whole is crucial.

Mapping is the process of setting the points out in a logical way with all the connections between them. We need to have the points in order to build the plan from A to B—it can't be done without them. If you say you'd "like to stop working someday," which is what many of our clients

want, that's too vague. There's actually no information
there to work with.

PRESCRIPTION WITHOUT DIAGNOSIS

Successful people are busy, and often they get wrapped
around the axle of the demands of daily life. They hav-
en't thought about why they're doing what they're doing.
Once we find clarity on what they want to do and what's
most important to them, we often discover that these
long-awaited dreams are within grasp, not in ten years,
but in ten months. Or, to a lesser extent, even tomorrow.
They're *that* close to what they want, but didn't know it.

Successful people aren't often all that happy, and they
aren't living the lives they want, because they've never
taken the time to define what that means and what that
looks like. It's so tempting—given the media's obsession
with methods and the constant demands of everyday
life—to focus on the trivial. They've never had a conversation with their family about values. They have no clear
set of goals. It's an incredibly useful conversation for your
family, not just your finances, by the way. Establishing
those values brings in an incredible focus, which makes
it easier to make decisions across the board.

Guiding our clients through this process is often frus-
trating for them—given that they often just want a quick

answer—but it's the most valuable thing we do. It's impossible to get you to a great outcome until we understand ultimately what outcome you want. How can we possibly give you a prescription without diagnosing your real problem? And yet, that's what people in this industry do every day—often to the client's detriment.

In a lot of cases, clients think they want one thing and end up deciding they actually want something else. Once we had a physician come in wanting to know if he should buy or lease the new car he wanted. As part of our discovery process, we asked, "Is there anything important for you outside of your family, your business, and your charity?" He ended up telling a story about working with Doctors Without Borders in a small village. He'd spent all day in the rain, hiking up a muddy mountain to get to this one village to take care of the kids there. By the time he arrived, it was midnight, and he took off his boots and put them outside his tent. When he woke up, his boots were gone. When he exited the tent, he saw his boots sitting ten feet away, freshly cleaned and drying in the sun. One of the children who lived there had taken his boots to the bottom of the mountain to clean them and brought them back to dry.

The doctor was crying as he told the story. "That moved me more than probably my entire career of medicine has up to this point." After the story, he found that he desperately wanted to have the kind of flexibility to make that kind of impact on people again in the future.

He asked how he could get there, and I circled back to his original question. How important was buying or leasing a car in the context of this larger discussion of impact? He told me it wasn't important at all, so we spent the rest of our time together that day figuring out the path to his real goal of helping those in need.

DOCTOR OR DRUG DEALER?

We always spend the time to diagnose, even if it irritates the client. A doctor can't prescribe without diagnosing. I can't walk into a doctor's office and say, "I want some Adderall." If that doctor gives me the prescription without diagnosing me, he is no longer a doctor; he's a drug dealer. In my world, financial drug dealers are wildly prevalent. People call their financial advisor and say they need such and such, and the advisor gives it to them without a blink of an eye! That's not a CFO, and that's not a partner.

A CFO takes the time to discover your real drivers and map out your real goals. Otherwise, you're shooting in the dark. No one can make great decisions if the decisions aren't anchored in what you really want.

WHERE ARE YOU NOW?

Once you've defined your goals, it's time to focus on where you are now. In the airport example, it's difficult to buy a ticket if you don't know where you're starting. Similarly, you have to understand your financial statements, your balance sheet, your income statement, and so forth. Most people don't understand these. Some people don't even know what they are! Without this kind of basic quantifiable information, it's impossible to move forward.

I've been in meetings where a client couple thinks they know where they are, where their point A is. Once I write it up on the whiteboard and start circling one thing and another, that's when husband and wife both look at it and suddenly start talking about their dad's house they inherited up in Colorado, or the apartment complexes they forgot to mention, or the CD they've been rolling over for years. Seeing your information in visual form unlocks your brain, and it gives you a chance to see and interact with the information in entirely new ways.

If a client's value is family, they will talk about spending more time with their grandkids and great-grandchildren. I'll ask what "more time" means, and they will talk about going on vacation with them. By the end, we would have drilled down to the fact that the client has dreamed about owning a lake house big enough for their whole extended family to come visit twice a year. There we go! Now we have a tangible goal we can plan toward.

I love having meetings with couples. The wife will remind the husband of his dreams, and vice versa.

"Honey, you've always wanted to have an art studio in the house because you love to draw!"

Inevitably he'll say that's not realistic.

"Why not?" we'll ask.

At that stage, we brainstorm everything—and I mean absolutely everything—and then ask two pertinent questions: What's most important? And then: What's most important *right now*? These are both important questions because the answers frame the map.

Mapping is hard. Often, even successful people haven't thought like this before. It's also uncomfortable to say dreams and aspirations out loud because it makes them feel real, and if we then don't achieve those dreams, we view it as failure. There's a fear involved in admitting to yourself that you have things that are important to you. From the outside perspective, though, we all only get one chance at life. Everything people want to accomplish is within their reach, if they just say it out loud and prioritize.

Prioritizing is also hard, but I find that if we focus on the one thing that can have the most impact on a client's life, the rest falls into place. Once we get to the most important, tangible goal, it's all numbers—just math and time. With computing power and technology, and with people who specialize in an area, solving problems is rarely the hard part. The hard part is asking the right questions, and defining where you are and where you want to go. We have to have the right inputs to get outputs that mean anything at all.

Living out your dreams starts with knowing what your dreams are.

CLEAR VISUAL COMMUNICATION

Mapping makes a huge difference. To show you how, let's contrast a good map with a densely written, ninety-page document. With the ninety-page document, the client's eyes glaze over, and half the professionals' do too. No one fully understands exactly what's meant by certain sections. The client doesn't understand it, and certainly doesn't understand or care how it relates to their situation.

In contrast, the visual map ties all the components together in a way that's clear and concise. Everyone is literally on the same page. The client not only understands the topic and the goals, but now trusts the entire team to speak to her needs. The map represents the client's needs, ideas, wishes, and anxieties, in a way that makes the relationship between the pieces clear.

Imagine a spiderweb, where disturbing one thread shakes the whole web. At a certain level, as we've said, finances become both complex and interdependent. Having a picture of the web is a hundred times more useful when making decisions than trying to figure out the interdependencies with a checklist or a paragraph. Having the picture communicates clearly to the whole team what the client is about and how their situation stands. A picture forces the whole team to do what's called "radiant thinking."

Radiant thinking is a way of thinking by drawing (or seeing a drawing represented), where you start in the middle and write out the subject, then start branching out with thoughts and concepts. It's essential to represent the relationships between the ideas and then to group things in ways that make sense. Often, we'll start by grouping items in one way, and then the client will have me move some of them around until they group in a different way. It's easier to see blind spots visually, and to figure out what questions need to be asked.

I love this process. Not only does it engage the brain in new ways because most people better understand visual representations, but it's fun for me to see the process fold out with my clients. When I write down the names of my clients' kids—say John, Susie, and Harry—I start drawing circles and pointing arrows to them from the fund that's supposed to take care of the kids. Then, suddenly, the client stops me, telling me that they want that particular fund to take care of something else. Until we drew a picture, the brain didn't make the connection.

The pictures we end up with represent you in an easy-to-understand, intuitive way that we use to focus our efforts. It's a clear and shared understanding of where you are now and where you want to go—which takes us to the next step: the plan.

CHAPTER EIGHT

MAKE A PLAN

plan
/plan/
noun

1. a detailed proposal for doing or achieving something.

verb

1. decide on and arrange in advance.

Just as the word *map* could be used as both a noun and a verb, so can the word *plan*.

The plan, the noun, is a living to-do list. Given that we're going from LA (where we are now) to New York (where we want to go), we need a plan to travel there. What do we need to do in order to successfully arrive at our destination healthy and happy? Nothing in life is guaranteed, but there are things that can be done in both the short and the long term to give the best possible outcome, and an effective plan is necessary for that. Most importantly, it tells you what to do next.

People don't engage for a plan, a document; people engage for the action or implementation of the plan—*to plan*, as a verb. The simpler your plan, the more likely you are to implement it. Planning is the ongoing process of taking stock of where you are and figuring out the next thing you need to do to make progress on your map.

People often approach planning far too linearly, trying to draw a straight line across the map, rather than figuring out the tasks that need to be done next. On a transcontinental airplane, the airplane is almost never on course. The line across the ocean isn't where you are at any given moment, given wind streams and all the rest. But through constant course correction, over time the airplane travels exactly where it needs to (hopefully). It's the same with your finances. You're rarely exactly where you want to be at that moment, but with constant course correction, you get where you need to go.

ZEROING IN

If the visualization and the mapping part of the process are about brainstorming and gathering all the information, planning is about zeroing in on implementation. A CFO continues to prioritize, figures out what needs to be done, and then does it.

Defining what we need carefully and putting constraints in place is helpful at this stage. Once we've gone big, then we go small. Essentialism talks about circling the most important thing, and then making the circle smaller and smaller, dissecting it until we find out what's the most important thing *right now*.

When you're identifying any goal, most people are typically going to have more than one thing they want to accomplish. Perhaps it is being financially independent, making sure they don't run out of money, and taking care of their kids. By zeroing in, a CFO helps to identify the most important goal. Then the CFO helps to identify what's the most important thing *right now*.

Then we apply the process of planning to identify the steps needed to accomplish the goal. In the long term, there will be some checkpoints we'll need to hit. In the short term, there will be a set of specific things we'll need to start moving on today. If we're trying to get somewhere in twenty years, we can't start on year twenty today. Instead, we start by asking: Given the twenty-year goal, where do we need to be in ten years? Where do we need to be in five, three, and one? What do we need to do now?

We start big, and then we go small and specific, always referring back to the map we built beforehand.

THE RIGHT FOCUS

One of the most critical stages of this process is choosing the right goal, and the right actions that will make the most difference. What is going to have the most impact on your happiness? What do you want the most? Focusing on the right thing is critical, because there's only so much energy to go around. Decision fatigue and information overload happen just as easily with too many goals as with too many choices. That's why the values and mapping exercises are so important. Rather than spending our limited energy on unimportant things, like the car lease or purchase, we spend them on the important stuff, like the impact the client felt through Doctors Without Borders.

Once we know what to focus on, we have to narrow even further to what specific items to do. In theory, we could make laundry lists of two hundred things to do on any given project. The art of planning is focusing in on the most important, high-impact things. What three to five things can give us the most impact today, if we only tackled those three to five things? Then we start crossing off the list, and when things get crossed off, we add more high-impact items.

When we're talking about mapping, there are no wrong answers. Whereas I've had some clients say they want to spend every penny of what they have while they're alive, I've had others say they want to limit spending because they want every penny to go to their children. Neither is wrong.

Whereas we wanted to focus on radiant thinking with mapping, for planning it's important to spend some time with linear thinking. Most likely our journey won't be a straight line; like the airplane course example, we'll have to course correct a hundred times because of prevailing winds. Some people will also choose to go through Paris for a two-day layover on their way to Rome, for example, rather than take a nonstop.

Linear thinking emphasizes sequences, meaning first we do this, then we do that, in a sequential way. Linear planning means focusing on the order of what needs to be done as we prioritize and implement. Unless something dramatically changes, we don't do year-five projects until we've completed year-one projects.

CHANGE IS INEVITABLE

When we're talking about a plan, it's important to note that this is a living document, something that will change as life changes. You want to have made your core plan, your baseline, so that you'll have an idea of what to change as circumstances change to still get what you want. As Mike Tyson said, "Everybody's got a plan until they get punched in the mouth." The process of how to change your plan becomes as important as the plan you make.

Your destination doesn't change, but conditions do! Any good plan (and process of adjusting your plan) will allow for those changing conditions.

When I'm driving from point A to point B, I don't give up just because there's a traffic accident. Even if there are many accidents, there are always detours. Financial plans are like that; you have to build some wiggle room mentally, because you don't know what's going to happen. Bear markets are as common as traffic accidents blocking your way.

PRIORITIZING FOR PROGRESS

It's tempting to run after too many goals, but when we try to move in several directions at once, we get nowhere. We accomplish little, if anything. Whereas, when we focus on one goal, and specifically on the tasks that get us the farthest, we make meaningful progress.

Referring back to the circle of essentialism, what is the most important thing right now? If you want to retire in twenty-five years on a beach in Miami and spend your time chasing the grandkids, we'll ask: What is the most important thing to do *right now* to make that happen?

The plan is the specific steps that need to happen to get us there. We know down the road there will be a list of things we'll have to do that we can't necessarily predict. We don't know what the winds will be like then, but we can set goalposts that give us the best likelihood of success.

Another way to think about priorities is by putting them in urgent and important quadrants. They're organized in one of four options: urgent, important; urgent, not important; not urgent, important; and not urgent, not important. People often go around tending to the urgent but not important, such as the buy-or-lease-a-car question from the man who valued the Doctors Without Borders experience.

SIMPLER IS BETTER

As we talked about in chapter 1, we want to keep things as simple as possible, but not simpler. In a situation where there are two possible explanations, Occam's razor says the simpler one is usually correct. It's almost always worth assuming the simpler scenario (even in an imprecise world) because fewer variables make planning easier. The potential outcomes and our understanding of them is clearer. Since clarity and confidence go hand in hand, when we keep things simpler, we're happier.

This seems like common sense. Most of us realize that simpler is better except when we come face-to-face with complex options, but *common sense isn't common* and *simple isn't always easy.*

Financial planning is both an art and a science. There's the science part, with numbers and formulas, behavioral science, and financial mathematics. There's also the art portion (which we saw in the mapping stage) of discovering where we are, where we want to go, and some of the terrain and decisions in between. There's also a portion that's about managing trade-offs; in a lot of situations, we're forced to use different levers—spend more now to push off goals, for example.

I DRIVE, YOU DRIVE

Many of our clients need to make complex financial decisions with lots of moving parts. The client–CFO relationship thus has an "I drive, you drive" component in each meeting. It's not just one person talking at the other for an hour; it's a collaborative experience.

The *I drive* is what the CFO needs to get from you in order to make sure he is making the best decisions, because certain things need to happen no matter what. It's focused on talking about your Point A: Where are you now? Any time you meet with your financial team, there's going to be a component where they need to do certain things on your behalf. You will have made progress, so the CFO needs to make sure to understand where that progress has taken you. That way, he can make sure your balance sheets and financial statements are updated since your Point A is always moving.

Then there's going to be the part where *you drive*, where you can control that agenda and talk about what's most important to you. Talk about anything that might be bugging you. It's an open forum; talk about whatever you want to talk about.

In meetings, the CFO brings up those small issues the client needs to deal with. Then the client knocks out the things they want to accomplish, and drives some of the priorities of what happens next. The conversations become less about how things work and more about how they work together—according to the plan.

SMALL WINS ADD UP

Small, consistent action makes huge progress over time. Many people try to focus on the moon shots—the unlikely, pie-in-the-sky, big-return ideas that may or may not happen. What we can't forget about, however, is roof shots. Roof shots are smaller and attainable through systematic, daily action. They aren't nearly as glamourous, particularly in the short term.

Gradual, meaningful progress isn't glamorous, but it builds momentum, and momentum leads to success. If there's an elephant to eat, you have to do it one bite at a time. You also want to see that you're making progress; that's how even the hardest things become enjoyable— when you see you're making headway.

In the next chapter, we create check-ins with our clients regularly, so they can see that we're on track and doing great. That's why we set long-term, medium-term, and short-term goals, to give that sense of checking boxes. People like to get things done, like you do in a game; it's motivating, and it makes things more fun. You become empowered for the right reasons. Knowing what you need to do next, and all you need to do next, gives you clarity and focus and makes it more fun.

BUILD THE FOUNDATION

Give me six hours to chop down a tree and I will spend five hours sharpening the ax.

—ABRAHAM LINCOLN

If you're building a skyscraper, you're not going to start at ground level. You have to dig the foundations down into the earth. The foundation of your relationship with your CFO, as well as the foundation of mapping and planning, takes time. The time is more than worth it, when it comes time to start building up, because it takes more weight, and when the wind blows, the building won't fall down.

We see a lot of clients whose foundation is in the sand. They're only focused on investments and building walls of decisions without any foundation of values or mapping at all.

The goal of an effective planning process, in contrast, is to have clearly defined objectives for you and the CFO to focus on. You know where the focus should be. If you're building your house, you might want to have a weekly meeting with your contractor to have a walk-through of the project's status. A lot happens behind the scenes between weekly meetings, probably more than you see, as issues arise and are dealt with. But you *can* see the progress being made.

While your planning process should be clear and as simple as possible, realize that if your financial world is complex, there will be a huge number of moving parts being handled for you behind the scenes, like a duck on water. You'll see the duck sailing smoothly along on top of the water, graceful and calm. Meanwhile, his feet are paddling madly underwater.

As the CFO starts working through a plan and her legs start paddling underwater, she checks in with the client a few times to talk about what she's seeing in the numbers, and whether the client would prefer to choose path A or path B. In finance, there are trade-offs between now and later, and it's always worth having a conversation about those decisions in terms of specifics. A CFO won't offer fifteen options, because given the right inputs and the map, there are often only a couple of options that fit the client's objectives.

COOL AND CALM

As we go through the planning process, it's important to talk about variables before they happen. As we said earlier with the car accident and detour example, every journey will have some challenges. Bear markets happen every five to seven years—they're common, and we have to plan for them.

Because we know these things are going to happen, we talk about them and plan for them ahead of time. Knowing that volatility will come—and having a plan for it—makes people feel more comfortable, and that helps them make better decisions in a cool, calm state while the rest of the world loses their minds. It's in those moments of volatility that some of the best gains can be made because so few people are thinking clearly; in finances, other people's bad decisions can often be to your benefit.

I also remind my clients to ignore CNBC, *Money Magazine*, and the rest of the information overload out there because market volatility will happen—and none of it affects whether they can afford to send their grandkids to college, take that trip to India, or give to their favorite charity. We assure them of this frequently, and to further help ease any worries, we offer several ways of measuring their progress, which we'll dive into in the next chapter.

CHAPTER NINE

MEASURE

Trust, but verify.

—RONALD REAGAN

The relationship with your CFO has to be built on trust so that you're not always worrying. I know it's often difficult for successful people to trust someone else to handle their money because they're used to being the one in control. But by delegating things outside of their core competency, they free up an incredible amount of time and energy to focus on other things. In order to delegate these things to someone else who specializes in them, however, they have to trust that CFO.

One of the advantages of setting benchmarks with the CEO and CFO together is there are built-in ways for the CEO to tell if the CFO is doing their job. There is a systematic way to verify that you are on track. The CFO can report the metrics and then have a discussion about progress. Are we on track? Are we off track? Why or why not, and what are the next steps? Your personal CFO is accountable for helping you achieve your goals.

What are the things we look at to measure success? Do we mean net growth at this rate, net earnings at this rate, savings per month, or something else entirely? Choosing the right numbers means that even if you were on a desert island and all you saw was a printout with the metrics, you'd know what you needed to know about how you're doing financially. These metrics are our family scorecard.

Choosing the right metrics becomes part of the mapping and planning process, and the choice of metrics is something that normally stays the same over time—and because they're attached to your core values, they're meaningful. You understand how they're attached to your goals, and you can look at them and quickly understand how well or poorly you're doing. Then you can decide what kind of conversation to have with the CFO about it, and how much time you want to spend going into the weeds to find out what, if anything, has gone wrong.

Having the metrics and benchmarks helps the successful person trust the CFO, and helps them see what's going on in a simple, but useful way. It becomes part of the rhythm of managing their success. For some clients, that means quarterly check-ins; for others, monthly; still others prefer to have the dashboard where they *can* look at their metrics at any time, but rely on us to call them if something comes up. It becomes very much about what's most useful for the individual.

In the beginning, typically our clients want to be more involved as it takes more thrust to get the airplane off the ground. As the plane's in the air and the airstream is smooth, and as we've worked together long enough that there's trust built, the client goes back to focusing on their normal day-to-day activities. As long as there aren't any big changes, it's not something they want to spend a lot of time on.

When something goes off track more than the usual variances, it's the CFO's job to bring it to your attention. There's always a conversation about whether it's an expected fluctuation of the market or whether this represents a true problem. If it's a true problem, how do we respond? The CFO needs to clearly articulate why we're off track and what needs to be done to get back on track. Sometimes (very rarely) it's about adjusting the metric. More often it's about adding more steps or changing the way certain actions are taken.

A scorecard or dashboard includes not only your individual metrics, but some standard indicators. One of these standard indicators is a net worth report, meaning your balance sheet, assets, and liabilities (you should be looking at these financial statements periodically). Your net worth gets better both when you pay down liabilities and when you build up assets. Are you going in the right direction over time?

VITALS

In meetings, the CFO drives the meeting by looking at the hard financials, the income statement, and the balance sheet. How are we doing on the statements? Then the client drives by setting the specific goal and the next most important thing to focus on for that goal.

Think of it as checking your financial health. When you go to the doctor for a check-up, she takes your vitals: your cholesterol, blood pressure, heart rate, and so on. These are all numbers that tell the doctor how your body is doing at this moment and where your trends are headed. Your financial statements are like your vitals, and similarly, if they get too far off what's expected, the CFO will have a conversation with you about what you need to do to get back on track. Your CFO should have a clipboard with your vitals (your balance sheet, your income statement, and what are the absolute, most important things for you to accomplish) and know this information at all times.

While you're at the doctor's office, you talk about your goals and ask how your health is going to affect those goals. Let's say you wanted to run a marathon, for example. Are you healthy enough? Can you train aggressively, or do you need to plan to take two years to build up to that point? Without your vitals, your doctor has no framework with which to advise you on what you need to do to hit your goals.

A good financial scorecard provides relevancy (meaning the vitals you're looking at matter to you) and clarity (meaning you know what you're looking at). Both together give you the confidence that you're on top of the financials, even as the CFO handles your day-to-day financial issues.

CONCLUSION

My wife and I went to Italy a few years ago and spent a few days in Florence and a few days in Rome. We planned the trip ourselves, and we enjoyed it immensely. My parents also visited Italy, but they opted for an all-inclusive, guided tour where you have flexibility to do what you want, but they also have things set up for you included in the price. My parents ended up attending a private party where they made pasta from scratch; they took a private tour to the symphony hall where a pianist played just for their group; and they ate at excellent restaurants and visited other hidden gems off the beaten path.

Day to day, they weren't thinking about which train to get on or where to go next; it was all handled for them. They relaxed and enjoyed the trip in a way that my wife and I didn't. My wife and I literally stumbled into the Pantheon.

We didn't know what we didn't know. Even though my trip was fun, it was also stressful at times as we tried to navigate a foreign landscape with limited knowledge.

Einstein talked about the eighth wonder of the world as compounding, but it can go both directions: up and down. It's easy in the financial world to make a small mistake that turns into a huge one over time. Years of good or bad decisions add up, and you can't go back to redo them. When it comes to your finances, you'll get to choose your own journey. What do you want to spend your time on?

FINDING A CFO

When you're looking for a CFO, ask first about the process they use. Is it a defined process? How much will they ask you about your values and goals, or in other words, what is their discovery process? Ask about the catalyst, advocate, and integrator roles. What is the CFO's experience in each, and how will they act in that capacity?

Talk about mapping, planning, and measuring. How do they handle these tasks? What's the process for deciding what's most important, and what's most important right now? How are plans made and goalposts decided on? How do they measure progress? Have them show you some examples.

Ask, "What happens if my finances get off track?"

A lot of people will ask a potential CFO about returns almost immediately. The litmus test between a good CFO and a bad one is the good one will respond as if this is a trick question. "If I don't know the goal, I can't define the method. What are your goals?" A bad candidate will answer the question with numbers and predictions. No one can predict the market, and therefore no one can accurately and consistently predict what the returns would be. You want a thinking partner, not a drug dealer. Thinking partners want to understand your *why*.

A key part of finding the right CFO is "fit." Is this a person you'll be comfortable sharing private financial information with? Does it feel right? Can you trust this person? When you talk to them, is it about you or is it about them? It needs to be about you.

ONE CFO

People can't have deep relationships with twenty financial people. It becomes too complicated. Too many advisors means no real advisors. The CFO is not a deep expert in a particular financial field; *the CFO should be an expert in you.* That means that he or she has to be enough of a financial generalist to handle all the experts working for you and handle all the moving parts at a high level. The experts are interchangeable. They come in and out of your life as needed. The CFO knows you and will learn everything he can about you before diagnosing and pre-scribing what you need.

TAKEAWAYS

Values and goals come before methods, so it's critical to understand where you want to go before you try to get there. Create a map, build a plan, and measure your progress. Work with a CFO you can trust, and enjoy your life. Remember that information overload leads to decision fatigue, so having a tight, limited focus makes everything else easier. Get the right inputs, because without the right inputs the outputs are ineffective.

And remember: it's *okay* not to want to manage your own personal wealth. Take back the one thing in life that is irreplaceable and that money can't buy: time. Whether that's more time with your cherished loved ones, more time traveling the world, more time picking up those hobbies you never got around to earlier in life, or more time enjoying the little things, like a good book or an excellent meal.

You don't have to be an expert. Instead, be the CEO of your life, and allow a CFO to handle the rest.

ABOUT THE AUTHOR

KYLE WALTERS, CFP®, CPWA®, CIMA®, is the founder of Atlas Wealth Advisors and L&H CPAs and Advisors, which specialize in helping entrepreneurs, physicians, executives, and retirees simplify their financial lives. He's been featured in *The Wall Street Journal* and on Fox TV, NBC, *The Dallas Morning News*, WealthManagement.com, and in Accounting Today. He lives in Dallas with his wife and two daughters.

86465777R00090

Made in the USA
San Bernardino, CA
28 August 2018